Purinton
POTTERY

Susan Morris

COLLECTOR BOOKS
A Division of Schroeder Publishing Co., Inc.

The current values of this book should be used only as a guide. They are not intended to set prices, which vary from one section of the country to another. Auction prices as well as dealer prices vary and are affected by condition as well as demand. Neither the Author nor the Publisher assumes responsibility for any losses that might be incurred as a result of consulting this guide.

Searching for a Publisher?

We are always looking for knowledgeable people considered to be experts within their fields. If you feel that there is a real need for a book on your collectible subject and have a large comprehensive collection, contact us.

Collector Books
P.O. Box 3009
Paducah, Kentucky 42002-3009

On the Cover:
Top left: HUMPTY DUMPTY Cookie Jar $450.00
Top right: PENNSYLVANIA DUTCH Jug $100.00
Bottom: APPLE Canister Set $240.00

Cover Design by Beth Summers
Book Design by Terri Stalions

❧ Contents ❧

❧ Acknowledgments ❧

With love and appreciation, I wish to express my gratitude to Blair and Doris Purinton, who shared valuable information and first-hand accounts regarding Purinton pottery production. Stepping into their home took us back to the days of the pottery trade, from being served lunch on a set of Intaglio dinnerware to sitting around in the family room looking over old newspaper clippings and photos and listening to stories about Blair's father and his company. I thank them not only for their wonderful friendship but for giving us the personal side of this remarkable story!

Special thanks goes to William "Bill" Bower whose technical expertise and superior memory provided much valuable information in the compilation of the history of the Purinton Pottery Company.

My heartfelt gratitude goes to Jim Schulte and Lori Hinterleiter, editors of *Purinton Pastimes*, who not only spurred my interest in Purinton pottery, but generously supplied information and pictures for this book.

My gratitude and admiration goes to Pat Dole, author of a former publication about Purinton pottery, who is probably responsible for the initial interest in the pottery and whose research we are grateful for.

This book was made possible by the generous cooperation of many collectors and dealers, including: Paul Moore; Marcy Cheke, Ron & Carol Harris, Clarion Antique Mall; Ora & Joanne Beary; Jerry and Cathee Anderson; John and Kristin Noveske; Gary & Starla Purinton; Dixie Enyeart; Pat & Kris Secor, Olde Central Antique Mall; Jim and Jan Seeck; Jerel Lenfestey; Joseph McManus; Tony Powell; Warren & Kay Chapman; Julie Cappiello; Jim Schulte and Lori Hinterleiter, *Purinton Pastimes*.

A very special thanks to the crew at Ames Photo in Mason City, IA for their patience and skill in developing my photographs which were many times taken in less than desirable conditions.

For technical information and/or photographs, thanks to: Michael Bertheaud, Clarion County Historical Society; Carol Cox, Smithsonian Institute, Ceramics and Glass Division; *The Clarion Republican*; *The Oil City Blizzard*; *The Forest Republican*; *Jamestown Post-Journal*; *The Crockery and Glass Journal*.

And last, but not least, special thanks and appreciation to my husband, Dave, and my three sons, Damon, John, and Aaron for putting up with wall-to-wall pottery and generously sharing my time and attention while writing this book.

Pattern names assigned by the Purinton Pottery Company:

Peasant Ware	Apple	Fruit	Seaform
Provincial Fruit	Intaglio	Heather Plaid	Ming Tree
Normandy Plaid	Maywood	Saraband	Tea Rose
Pennsylvania Dutch	Chartreuse	Palm Tree	Harmony

Pattern names assigned by Pat Dole:

Ivy	Petals	Sunny	Shooting Star
Crescent	Ribbon Flower	Windflower	Cherries

Other pattern names were assigned by the author for identification purposes.

❦ Foreword ❧

Purinton pottery captured my attention a couple years ago while doing research for my book on Watt pottery. Handcrafted ware from the 1940's and 1950's is so typically "American" and reminds us of a time when an emphasis was placed on hospitality in the home. The hand-painted art work applied to these lovely pieces is reminiscent of a time that was unhurried, where quality, value, and tradition were the bywords of skilled craftsman and artisans.

It has been a real adventure discovering the wide array of patterns and shapes that Purinton created, many never previously identified as their pottery before. My sincere hope is that your journey through the pages of this book will be as much of an adventure, and that your collecting endeavors will be most gratifying and enjoyable.

Susan Morris

How to Use
❧ This Identification and Value Guide ❧

The Purinton Pottery Company produced a vast assortment of molds in various patterns, and for this reason not all pieces which were produced could be photographed and valued. This book will serve as a guide in identifying molds and patterns produced by Purinton and will give the collector or dealer a general value guide for a wide assortment of pieces, both common and rare.

Dimensions given are approximations and widths, heights, or diameters listed are measured at the widest or highest point, unless otherwise noted. Please note that measurements may vary slightly due to factory run inconsistencies. Because of the off-round shape of many Purinton pieces, diameters given were measured between opposite corners on applicable items. Bottom markings are usually not noted, unless the piece has been hand-signed by the artist. See Chapter 14 for a discussion and photographs regarding company markings on the pottery.

Chapter 1 contains a general history of the pottery company and its founders. It also discusses the unique methods used by Purinton to create this delightful pottery, as well as a general introduction of the various pattern lines. Specific patterns are illustrated in each of the following chapters. Chapter 2 illustrates pieces made in Purinton's early years at the Wellsville, Ohio plant. Chapters 3 through 10 cover the main dinnerware lines which were heavily produced and offered in open stock. Chapter 11 deals with many miscellaneous short-run series as well as novelty or specialty items, souvenir pieces, and figural cookie jars. Chapter 12 illustrates many rare and possibly one-of-a-kind items, while Chapter 13 shows examples of private mold work contracted for other companies.

Although there is no definite value for any collectible, this price guide is intended to help the collector or dealer determine an approximate measure of value for a particular piece. The prices listed in this guide reflect the input of many collectors and dealers. However, because of the wide variety of patterns and shapes offered in the Purinton line, what appeals to one collector may not appeal to another, and so personal preference may play an important part in determining the value of a particular piece. Prices may vary according to geographical location and this guide reflects an average evaluation of these fluctuations.

The values in this guide assume that the piece is in mint condition, lids intact, even though the photographed item may not be. In instances of particularly rare pieces, a plus (+) may be added to the value given to indicate high desirability and inflationary tendencies.

Purinton Pastimes
A collectors newsletter for Purinton Pottery enthusiasts.

$10.00 for a one-year subscription (four issues per year)
Write to:
Purinton Pastimes
P.O. Box 9394
Arlington, VA 22219

Chapter 1

❧ The History of Purinton Pottery ❧

In the Beginning — The Founding of a Pottery

Since as early as 1840 the name "Purinton" has been connected with the pottery business. The manufacture of pottery in the United States began in East Liverpool, Ohio with crude utility ware crafted from local clays. Since that time the district became a center for the production of ware and led in the discovery of pottery advancements.

A family which lived in East Liverpool, Ohio and was influential in its business life was the Purintons. Bernard Purinton came from this long line of pottery specialists and, as a result of his inventive persistence, evolved a unique pottery casting process and a ware unequalled in distinction and beauty.

It was by the efforts of many people that Purinton pottery came to be. Let us introduce you to some of the people that were significant in the creation of this unique ware.

Bernard Purinton ❧

Bernard Purinton was born in East Liverpool, Ohio and literally devoted his life to the pottery industry. After taking classes in ceramics at Ohio State University, he was employed by the East Liverpool Potteries Company, manufacturers of dinnerware and semi-porcelain specialties, and for a number of years held the position of general manager. The company liquidated in the early 1930's and Purinton decided to devote all of his energies to the development of a mechanical casting process which he believed to have great possibilities in the future of the pottery industry. With the help of a few associates and his own capital, Purinton devoted the next five years to

Bernard Purinton

research. His vision was to perfect and patent a method in which pottery of a distinctive design would be produced quickly and economically in a wholesale production line.

In 1936 Purinton became the owner of a Wellsville, Ohio pottery plant and named it the Purinton Pottery Company. The Purintons produced a pottery in the form of salad sets, coffee and tea sets, Tom and Jerry combinations, and special decorative pieces with lovely hand-painted designs which they referred to as "Peasant Ware."

By 1940, having secured patents on his unique casting process and realizing that the Wellsville plant was not geared to the quantity and quality production he desired, Bernard Purinton began seeking a location for a new and improved pottery manufacturing plant. There was a sharp decline of imported ware into this country, and Purinton, with his vast knowledge of the pottery industry and his patented ideas, wanted to be prepared for the expanding pottery industry in the United States.

His search led him to Clarion County, Pennsylvania. The area could offer the facilities he needed for a new plant such as utilities, railway siding, and approach from the highway. But more than anything, Purinton was impressed with the enthusiasm and support of the leading businessmen of the area. The Clarion County Chamber of Commerce, the Shippenville Men's Club, and many other organizations and individuals entered the scene at this point and persuaded Purinton to locate his new plant in the small town of Shippenville, five miles west of Clarion, Pennsylvania. Due largely to the efforts of an energetic and cooperative community, the new Purinton plant was open for production on December 2, 1941. This 30,000 square foot plant was laid out and equipped to meet the rigid requirements of Purinton's new pottery casting method. It housed the factory, warehouse, casting room, kiln, and shipping department and would employ 75 to 100 people at full capacity. Bernard Purinton's dreams were being fulfilled and the next 18 years proved the Purinton Pottery to be a pioneer in the mass production of free brush underglaze ware.

The Purinton Pottery plant in Shippenville, Pennsylvania

William J. Bower ⚕

William "Bill" Bower, resident of Knox, Pennsylvania, was the secretary of the Clarion County Chamber of Commerce at the time of the relocation of the Purinton Pottery Company. This energetic and efficient member of the community worked diligently to rehabilitate the economy of Clarion County, Pennsylvania by bringing in this new pottery industry. In April, 1941 he was named Secretary-Treasurer of the new company and was placed in charge of office and management detail. He worked closely with Bernard Purinton in the fulfillment of his vision of a modern pottery production unit.

John M. Hammer ⚕

John M. Hammer was named sales manager of the new Purinton Pottery Company in Shippenville. Not only was he responsible for bringing Roy Underwood and the Clarion County Chamber of Commerce into contact with Bernard Purinton, but his vast experience in the pottery industry proved invaluable in the fulfillment of Purinton's dream. For many years editor of many trade journals in the pottery and glass industries, he was widely accepted as an authority in the field. He was a former president of the Western Glass and Potters' Association and was among the organizers of the Associated Glass and Pottery Manufacturers. For 20 years Hammer was manager of the Pittsburgh Glass and Pottery Exhibit, a popular trade show held for retailers in Pittsburgh, Pennsylvania since 1880. John Hammer was an important link between the Purinton production line and the pottery salesmen and buyers in the industry.

Purinton Pottery Company became an exhibitor at the Pittsburgh China and Glass Exhibit, a national trade show for retailers, through the efforts of John M. Hammer, show manager and executive secretary for Associated Glass and Pottery Manufacturers who were sponsors of the show. John L. Pasmantier & Sons were the eastern sales representatives who set up this booth at the show.

Roy R. Underwood ❧

The Purinton Pottery Company found its vice-president in Roy R. Underwood. He was from Knox, Pennsylvania, and was president of the Knox Glass Associates, Inc. and first president of the newly formed Clarion County Chamber of Commerce. His unique combination of skill, knowledge, vision, and initiative accounts for the fact that he was one of the first men to recognize the immense marketing potential for the pottery industry.

He worked alongside Bernard Purinton in making a thorough investigation of marketing possibilities and production challenges. He knew that Purinton's techniques would make possible a very profitable operation, and his foresight helped to make the dream a reality.

Dorothy Purinton ❧

Dorothy Purinton's roots were in Mt. Vernon, Ohio. She met Bernard Purinton on a blind date while attending college in Wooster, Ohio and they were married in 1917.

Dorothy never worked at the Wellsville, Ohio pottery plant and actually only worked part-time at the Shippenville, Pennsylvania plant. Having received no formal art education, her natural talent, as well as her loyal support, was an invaluable resource for her husband's business. Although she was never considered a salaried employee, Dorothy assisted her brother, William Blair in not only training the decorators, but in designing the patterns used on the ware. She is credited with the design of Intaglio, Maywood, Saraband, Pennsylvania Dutch, Tea Rose, and the many patterns that followed. Dorothy Purinton's creative ingenuity gave an innovative pottery its warmth and charm.

Dorothy Purinton visiting with her husband, Bernard, in the shipping room.

Dorothy Purinton decorating MOUNTAIN ROSE two-cup teapots for the McCormick Tea Company.

William H. Blair ✆

William Blair, Dorothy Purinton's brother, played a significant role in the creation of Purinton pottery's bold and colorful look.

After attending the Cleveland Art Institute, Blair traveled throughout Europe studying art and doing portraits. However, when the Purinton Pottery Company opened in Wellsville, Ohio, Blair's interest in art soon expanded into the pottery industry as he became a key figure in his brother-in-law's new operation. His artistic background and talent layed the groundwork for the decorating phase of the Purinton pottery process. Blair is credited with the design of not only all of the Wellsville patterns, but the early Shippenville designs as well, among them the popular Apple and Plaids. He painted many unusual, one-of-a-kind pieces, many of which bear his signature on the back or bottom. He was also influential in the design of Purinton's innovative off-round shapes.

Blair left the Purinton plant in 1945 to establish a pottery plant of his own, Blair Ceramics, Incorporated in Ozark, Missouri.

Blair Purinton ✆

Blair Purinton, son of Bernard and Dorothy, became quite familiar with his parents' new pottery business, working there part-time during his high school years. He attended Allegheny College, served in the U.S. Navy during World War II, and married his wife, Doris, in 1947. At that time he resumed his employment, working at both the Shippenville and Tionesta plants on a full-time basis.

Blair was a very adaptable employee who soon became fully acquainted with all facets of the business. He served in various capacities demonstrating proficiency in not only the management and sales phases of the operation, but also with his artistic capabilities in the decorating department as well. He helped train decorators when needed and was known to wield a paint brush himself from time to time.

The rare and highly sought after Purinton "butter dish" was inadvertently designed by Blair Purinton. As the company was known to design molds for private enterprises, he had originally designed the piece for an outsider to be used as a "drippings catcher" for a meat carving block. It was a difficult piece to produce even though it was manufactured on a Ram Press, which may explain the reason for its limited production.

Blair continued his work at the plant until 1959 when it discontinued operation.

Blair, Dorothy, and Bernard Purinton

Purinton Slip Ware — A Unique Pottery

The Purintons produced a pottery with lovely hand-painted designs on creamy white clay in many innovative shapes. Not only were they pioneers in the use of a wide variety of multicolored free brush patterns, but the design and form used for their molds were original and unique. Their dinner and breakfast plates were an off-round shape, never before seen in the industry. Much of the hollow ware was popularly identified by its shape rather than pattern, such as "Dutch jug," "Kent jug," "Honey jug," and "Rebecca jug."

In the early years at the Wellsville, Ohio plant the company produced coffee and tea sets, salad sets, and breakfast sets under the name "Slip Ware" and "Peasant Ware." Production and variety was rather limited at this point, most pieces bearing rather primitive motifs of fruits (apples, pears, grapes, and pineapples), floral designs, cactus designs, and peasant women (candleholders and oasis jug).

Upon relocation of the plant to Shippenville, Pennsylvania, production and variety were to increase dramatically. In the beginning only solid glaze ware was produced because the decorators had not yet been properly trained. A large contract with the McCormick Tea Company for a yellow two-cup individual teapot to be used in a tea premium giveaway promotion proved to be a disappointment. These yellow teapots were the first pieces to emerge from the kiln at the new plant on December 7, 1941, the day that Pearl Harbor was bombed. The scarcity of tea products during this time made it impractical to further a tea premium promotion and the contract was phased out. The teapots were ultimately sold to some chain stores throughout the country. Family members recall that the first 100 of these yellow teapots to be produced were inscribed by Bernard Purinton on the bottom "12-2-41 B.P.," the day they were cast.

It was at this point that Purinton decided to promote decorated lines of pottery. At a cost of only a few cents per piece, decorated ware would command double the price. There was also an interest in acquiring contracts for premium giveaways as big profits could be realized in that type of business. Gift and china shops, hardware stores, and chain stores were contacted and within the next few years Purinton pottery appeared in almost every major department store throughout the United States and Canada. It was even exported to such countries as Africa and Cuba. The Fruit pattern continued in production at the new plant, employing the solid apple and pear motif. Many specialty items were produced in this pattern including teapots, coffee pots, pitchers, canister sets, and range sets, however, it was never offered in a complete dinnerware set.

In the early 1940's William Blair designed the popular Apple pattern. Not only did this pattern prove to be the company's best seller but it is probably the most sought after by collectors today. This bold and colorful pattern was the first in a wide range of patterns to be offered in a full dinnerware line, along with an extensive selection of accessory pieces. All dinnerware lines were offered in either a 6-piece place setting, 16-piece starter set (service for four), 32-piece dinner set (service for six), or 53-piece dinner set (service for eight). Purinton dinnerware was produced as open stock and retailers could carry any segment of the complete line of over 45 different pieces.

Soon after the Apple line was in production, other patterns were developed, including the Intaglios and Plaids. By this time Dorothy Purinton, wife of Bernard Purinton, joined William Blair in teaching the decorators and is credited with designing all remaining patterns used, with the exception of the Plaids.

"Intaglio," which means "incised design," was the name given to William Blair's novel idea of incising a pattern into a background of brush-stroked color. While he experimented with the idea of incising animal designs and such, Dorothy Purinton is credited with the design of the main dinnerware line which featured a flower pattern incised into either a rich brown or blue-green back-

Have no fear about putting your Purinton Ware in your automatic dish washer.

• • • •

The decorations are applied on each item and then fired at high temperature so as to actually become a part of the piece itself. The colors you see are underneath the glaze and can never be harmed nor removed.

• • • •

Each piece is individually decorated with free hand brush strokes and, since no decals and no stencils are used, the result is a truly handcrafted product both in appearance and in quality. There is no monotonous mechanical feeling about Purinton hand decorations.

• • • •

No need to worry about putting your Purinton Ware right in the oven. Take it out of your oven and right to your table. No harm will be done to the deep rich colors.

• • • •

Whether it's dinner for guests, a quick lunch for two, or an outdoor picnic you are planning, you will like both the time you save and the compliments you get with your modern Purinton Service.

A brochure distributed by the Purinton Pottery Company listing some of the open stock items available.

	Open Stock Items		
No.	Item	No.	Item
60	Coffee Pot, 8 Cup	130	Dinner Plate
100	Teapot, 6 Cup	131	Ind. Bean Pot
101	Covered Sugar	133	Dessert
102	Creamer	134	Salad Bowl, 11″
105	Juice Pitcher, 2 Pt.	135	Covered Dish
107	Kent Jug, 1 Pt.	136	Salad Plate, 6¾″
108	Marmalade Jar	137	Vegetable, 8″
*109	Dutch Jug, 2 Pt.	139	Pickle Dish
*110	5 Pt. Beverage Jug	140	Baker, 7″
*111	Tumbler	*141	Spaghetti Bowl, 14½″
114	Jug Salt & Pepper	142	Meat Platter, 12″
*115	Juice Mug, 6 oz.	*143	Cookie Jar
116	3-Compt. Relish	145	Handled Mug, 8 oz.
117	Chop Plate, 12″	146	Beer Mug, 16 oz.
118	Fruit Bowl, 12″	151	Oil & Vinegar Jugs
125	Tea (Cup & Saucer)	83	Tea & Toast Set
126	Cereal-Soup Bowl	* 87	Range Set
127	Breakfast Plate	* 88	Canister Set

*Not available in all decorations

Manufactured by PURINTON POTTERY COMPANY, Shippenville, Pennsylvania

14

ground. The factory referred to the brown line as "Intaglio" and the blue-green line as "Turquoise." We have seen the Palm Tree pattern incised into backgrounds of royal blue, coral red, and shades of purple and a leaf design was incised into a carmel-colored background. However, these patterns are rare and were not offered in regular dinner line production.

The Intaglio patterns were introduced in a promotion of Purinton pottery through Bigelow's Department Store in New York in June, 1950. The Maywood pattern, designed by Dorothy Purinton, was also introduced at this time. It featured a large white dogwood flower on a greyish-green body.

The Normandy Plaid, designed by William Blair, was predominantly red with chartreuse and forest green accents. It was originally offered in a 16-piece starter set with 41 other open stock pieces. Heather Plaid made its debut as a "sister pattern" to the Normandy Plaid at the Pittsburgh Glass and Pottery Exhibit in December of 1951. It featured predominantly green color with red and yellow accents. We have also seen a few pieces in purple and carmel colors and assume these were merely experimental. Saraband, designed by Dorothy, was also introduced at this show with its graceful bands of forest green, chartreuse, and dark brown.

The Pennsylvania Dutch pattern was experimented with in the late 1940's and variations of its design can be found. However, the commonly known variation featuring either a pink heart or stylized tulip motif, or a combination of the two, became the pattern for a regular dinnerware line in the early 1950's. Production of this pattern was rather limited compared to the previously mentioned patterns and, because of its folk art look, it is extremely popular with collectors.

Other dinnerware patterns followed but were relatively limited in production and did not sell well. These included the elusive Tea Rose, Ming Tree, Seaform, Mountain Rose, Chartreuse, and others. Petals was a striking dinnerware line featuring a simple red and blue floral pattern that was produced for sale by Sears, Roebuck and Company. These and other patterns can be identified in the "Miscellaneous" chapter of this book.

Purinton fashioned many other patterns which were mainly used on hollow ware, such as the Ivy pattern with buds of either red or yellow. Large quantities of these novelty or specialty items were steadily produced and sold to chain stores. Many of the specialty items, such as small vases and planters, were decorated with various unnamed patterns and sold by the dozen to florist and gift shops. Containers were made for many kinds of products such as toiletries, condiments, and liquors. The "honey jug" was a container for honey used as a company premium in its initial production. Because Shippenville was considered the gateway to Cook Forest State Park, many souvenir pieces, some decorated with pine trees and log cabins, were made for restaurants and souvenir shops bearing the park's name.

One rather elusive pattern used for specialty ware was the Palm Tree, which was designed by Dorothy Purinton. These colorful pieces were produced specially for a souvenir and gift shop in Fort Meyers Beach, Florida, which was operated by John "Pete" Purinton, one of Bernard Purinton's sons. They are rare and command premium prices. John's wife, Kay, designed a line of primitive, but colorful hand-painted jewelry called Kay Kraft. Purinton also produced various hand-painted miniature figurines such as animals and shoes.

In addition to the regular lines, many individualized, sometimes one-of-a-kind pieces were produced such as plates and mugs for children or commemorative pieces made for anniversaries or other special events. The Autumn Leaf Festival was an annual event in the area for which Dorothy Purinton painted souvenir plates, very few of which were produced. Most of Dorothy Purinton's and William Blair's special pieces were dated and signed and are highly sought after by collectors. Examples of the above-mentioned pieces appear in Chapter 12. Employees of the Purinton Pottery Company were permitted to make unique and individual pieces for themselves, decorating them as they desired, sometimes adding their name.

This photo was taken at the Florida gift shop for which the PALM TREE line was designed. Notice the PALM TREE pieces on the middle shelf.

In the fall of 1948, as a result of efforts by Roy Underwood, a subsidiary plant was opened in the town of Tionesta, Pennsylvania, about 25 miles from the Shippenville plant. Purinton began contracting a considerable amount of private mold work for other companies and felt that a separate smaller plant would be more feasible for these production lines. However, all patterns and molds eventually became part of Tionesta's production line. The plant began operation with about 25 employees and was managed by Floyd Wills. It accommodated a "straight-away" kiln, as opposed to the circular kiln of the Shippenville operation.

Esmond Industries, Inc., a New York-based sales organization headed by Ben Asquith, is probably one of the most well known companies for which Purinton made pottery and their revolving canister set on a wooden base is a popular example. Purinton produced lazy susans, canister sets, and casseroles on stands for them. Pots, jardineres, and planters for florist shops were made for the National Potteries Corporation (NAPCO) of Cleveland, Ohio. The Rubel Company of New York designed their own molds for pottery production by the Purintons. The pieces made for Rubel had contemporary lines, were undecorated, and were usually glazed in solid color combinations of either black and white or brown and yellow. Purinton also did private mold work for Taylor, Smith, and Taylor (TS & T), a large pottery manufacturer in Chester, West Virginia. Many figural-type pieces were produced for them at the Tionesta plant, among them the rare and highly collectible Howdy Doody cookie jar and bank. Some of the pieces produced using NAPCO, Rubel and TS&T molds were decorated with "Purinton" patterns, but these were not part of a regular line and were usually sold locally. Some of these pieces are identified throughout this text. The business relationship established with Taylor, Smith & Taylor endured through the years as Bernard Purinton's niece married William "Bill" Smith III, one of the company owners. In 1958 the influx of foreign imports on the market caused considerable financial difficulties for the Purinton

Pottery Company. TS & T acquired a majority of the company stock and managed the plant until the pottery was liquidated in 1959.

The vivid, colorful patterns of this delightful pottery have captured the attention of many pottery collectors today. Although many pieces are plentiful, it is a challenge to discover the rare and unusual examples available. Its variety of patterns and unique shapes have helped place Purinton pottery high on the list of collectible pottery.

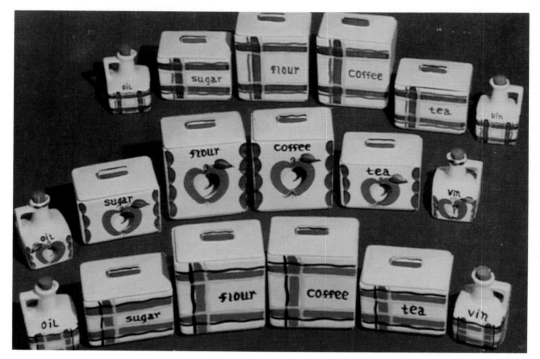

(Front)

Postcards illustrating various open stock items were distributed to prospective customers to spur pottery sales for the company. See also page 18.

POTTERY CANISTER SETS

Colorful canister sets in hand decorated colors on rich ivory toned pottery. Colors are fired underglaze and are absolutely permanent.

No. 88 Canister Set as illustrated .... $5.50 ea.

Packed 1 complete set in reshipping carton.

Available in three patterns illustrated

Heather Plaid (Top)   Apple (Center)   Normandy Plaid (Bottom)

Complete table service and a wide variety of casual serving pieces and gift items are also available in these same decorations. Price list will be sent on request.

PURINTON POTTERY COMPANY
Shippenville, Pennsylvania

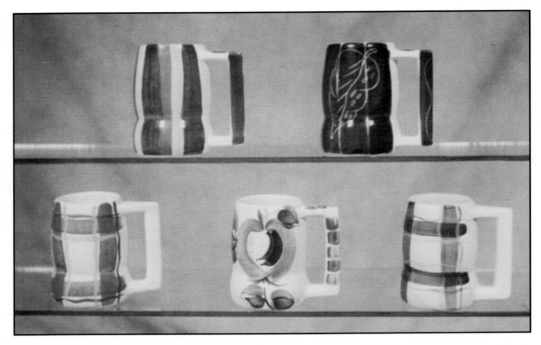

(Front)

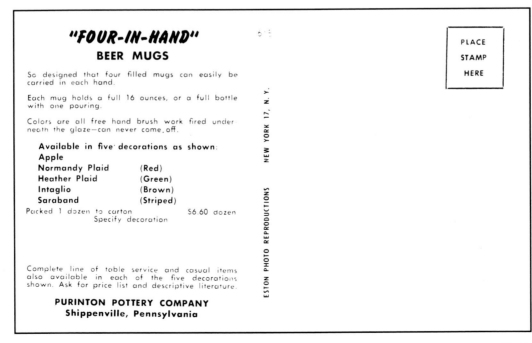

"FOUR-IN-HAND"
BEER MUGS

So designed that four filled mugs can easily be carried in each hand.

Each mug holds a full 16 ounces, or a full bottle with one pouring.

Colors are all free hand brush work fired underneath the glaze—can never come off.

Available in five decorations as shown:
Apple
Normandy Plaid   (Red)
Heather Plaid   (Green)
Intaglio   (Brown)
Saraband   (Striped)
Packed 1 dozen to carton $6.60 dozen
      Specify decoration

Complete line of table service and casual items also available in each of the five decorations shown. Ask for price list and descriptive literature.

PURINTON POTTERY COMPANY
Shippenville, Pennsylvania

ESTON PHOTO REPRODUCTIONS   NEW YORK 17, N. Y.

PLACE
STAMP
HERE

(Back)

18

The Purinton Casting Method

Purinton pottery's distinctiveness and individuality are manifest not only in its shape and design, but in the methods used to create it.

All mass produced pottery must begin with a working model and from this original design a mold is made. The first is the master mold and many molds are produced from the master. They were of two pieces and held together with rubber strips. These molds were made of plaster so they could absorb some of the water from the clay mixture which was poured inside.

All American dinnerware of this era was alike in that it was made of the same basic materials which are mixtures of clay in combination with feldspar and water. When these basic materials were mixed with water, the result was called slip. The Purintons used clays from Florida and Kentucky and feldspar from North Carolina. Local clays contained too much iron to be used in the pottery. The clay, feldspar, and other ingredients were measured and weighed in a conveyor using a carefully guarded formula developed through years of research and experiment. The material was then placed in mixing units where water was added. One of the factors that led to the selection of Shippenville as the pottery site was its iron-free water, which is an important ingredient in pottery production. At this point, the slip was forced through a press, extracting much of the water, resulting in large heaps of brownish material. These were again placed in mixing units and water added again. This slip went through three different agitators making sure the material was well mixed and of the proper consistency.

It was at this point that the Purinton's production system of hollow ware differed from any other pottery in the United States. Instead of the time-honored method by which a prescribed amount of slip is poured into each mold individually, a group of molds was immersed completely into a body of slip. Depending on size, between twenty and forty molds were placed on a wire rack which was eight feet long and four feet wide. The molds were placed in two rows using rubber spacers between them and a wooden wedge at each end to keep a tight fit. Seventy-eight 4-cup teapot molds could be held at one time on two trays. The wire tray holding these molds was suspended from an overhead trolley and the trays were advanced along this trolley to a position directly above a 17-foot tank. This tank was filled with about twelve inches of liquid slip and mounted on two hydraulic hoists. Being large enough to accommodate two of the mold-filled trays at one time, the tank was raised upward until the molds were completely submerged in the slip. The molds were positioned so that the slip openings were on the bottom and vented on the top to allow escape of air.

The Purintons cast the handles of pitchers and cups along with the main body of the piece, thus adding strength to the ware. Other potteries traditionally applied the handles and lids in a separate, time-consuming process. Another novel idea was casting a teapot and lid as one complete piece. The slip entered the mold through the spout area and air was allowed to escape through a vent at the outermost end of the handle. The teapot lid was part of the mold and was attached by means of a circular flange which was ¾" tall. When the moist ware was removed from the mold, the lid was cut off and the circular opening at the top of the teapot was smoothed off. About half of the flange that still remained on the lid was cut off and the rest was left on the lid to secure it firmly on the teapot when tilted. This procedure lended itself to mass production as it decreased the number of molds to be handled and simplified inventory control as each teapot always had its lid attached at the time of casting.

After being immersed in the slip for a period of about 15 minutes, the slip tank was lowered and excess slip was removed from the molds with a rubber scraper, allowing it to drip back into the slip tank.

The tray then moved onward along the trolley to an area where the molds and tray were cleaned completely with a high pressure sprayer. The Purinton molds were treated with a special coating including aluminum paint which not only controlled the drying time of the slip but allowed them to withstand this high water pressure.

It should be noted that some hand casting was done on larger pieces of ware. The slip was forced through nozzled hoses and poured into each mold individually. The molds could still be placed in rows on the movable trays for this procedure, however, they had to be positioned with the opening to the top instead of to the bottom as in the "one-dip" method. Also, the Purintons purchased a Ram Press in the mid-1950's for the fast, efficient molding of plates, butter dishes, and shallow bowls.

After a brief drying period, the molds were opened by hand, cleaned, and taken by conveyor to a large dryer to remove all moisture.

The cast ware at this point was still moist and extremely fragile. It was carted to an area where workers smoothed the rough edges and seams on the ware with knives and sponged them with water. After further drying, paraffin was applied to the bottoms of hollow ware pieces so that the glaze in the next procedure would not stick. Ware to be finished in plain glaze was trucked to an area where it was dipped in a glaze mixture of colors such as ivory, green, yellow, and brown. Pieces to be decorated by free-hand brush proceeded to the decorating department.

Workers cleaning and smoothing recently cast honey jugs. Notice the jug-style salt and pepper shakers in the foreground.

The workers here are making holes in the salt and pepper shakers as they had no holes in them when they came out of the mold. In a later operation toothpicks were stuck in the holes before dipping in the glaze in order to prevent them from being glazed shut.

The free-hand decorating procedure of Purinton Pottery was probably the most significant phase in its production as this is where the pieces took on their homespun flavor so loved by collectors today. Under the direction of Dorothy Purinton, a group of from eight to ten trained artisans painted designs on the ware using a solution of slip dyed with minerals to produce several warm, attractive colors. After the color dried, the ware was taken to the dipping department for a coat of white glaze. Then all articles, both plain and decorated, proceeded to the firing kiln.

Decorators free-hand brushed designs on the ware before the firing process.

A kiln is a large oven used to fire the glaze coating on the ware, thus sealing the color and design and making the piece both oven proof and dishwasher safe. Three hundred tons of brick and concrete were used to construct the large gas-powered, 70-foot kiln at the Purinton plant. Before entering the kiln, ware was placed in various-sized saggers, covered containers made of rough clay used to protect the ware from the direct flame of the kiln. The word "sagger" derives from the tendency of dishes to sag out of shape in the heat if not properly protected and supported. Hollow ware items were fired in oval-shaped saggers with sides about six to eight inches in height. Flatware items were fired in round shallow saggers with sides only two inches or so in height. More than one item could be placed in a sagger, depending on the size.

As was mentioned previously, many items were waxed on the bottom with melted paraffin before being dipped in the glaze solution. Any glaze solution adhering to the bottom over the wax was then wiped off before placing it in the sagger to be fired. The wax melted during firing leaving an unglazed bottom that would not stick to the sagger when it emerged from the kiln as a finished piece.

Over time, much of Purinton's ware was glazed on the bottom and had to be set on pins so as not to adhere to the bottom of the sagger during the firing process. These pins were thin ceramic sticks about two inches long, but were of a triangular configuration so they rested on the flat side with the top coming to a point. The pins were placed on the bottom of the sagger, three to each item, and were spaced to properly support the ware and keep it from touching the bottom of the sagger. Consequently, after firing, the glaze would properly adhere to the bottom of the piece except in the areas where the pins supported it. These spots would then be rubbed smooth with an abrasive stone.

The filled saggers were stacked on top of one another and placed on platforms atop a slowly moving, electrically powered conveyor system which travelled through the circular kiln. For at least one-third of this process, the ware was not being fired, but gradually heated in the beginning to reach a maximum temperature of 1900 degrees and then slowly cooled in the end. As each stack of saggers entered the kiln, another stack would be placed on the moving platform, keeping the kiln in full operation 24 hours a day, seven days a week. As the saggers emerged from the kiln, workers wearing protective gloves removed the fired ware and transported it to an area where "selectors" cleaned and inspected it, smoothed off the bottoms, and sent it to the shipping department for final selection and packing.

All procedures in the Purinton process were under rigid control and were acquired through much research and experimentation. Errors in drying and firing times could result in inferior quality. A retail outlet in Marianne, Pennsylvania called the Corner Cupboard was established to sell seconds from the plant.

The Purinton method produced a pottery light in weight but of unusual strength, pleasing to the eye yet serviceable. In kind and variety it was different from any other utility or serving ware of its time. It is truly a piece of Americana. From the materials and machinery used to form it to the ingenuity and skill of the craftsmen that created it, these American-made heirlooms with their down-home country flavor will be a favorite of collectors for years to come.

Chapter 2
Peasant Ware
✤ The Wellsville, Ohio Years ✤

The Purinton Pottery Company began producing free-hand decorated ware as early as 1936 in the form of salad sets, coffee and tea sets, and special decorative pieces which they referred to as "Peasant Ware." The colorful patterns, which were inspired by William Blair, were rather primitive in design and portray a folk art theme. Although this era of Purinton production is well-known for the "peasant" designs, other patterns using desert flowers and cactus scenes were produced under the Peasant Ware designation. Because the pattern designated as "Peasant Garden" originated at the Wellsville plant, all available photographs have been included in this chapter. However, most of the dinnerware line was produced at the Shippenville plant. It should also be noted that the Fruit pattern originated during this time. A few early pieces of Fruit are pictured in this chapter as they were produced in Wellsville. However, production of the Fruit pattern continued at the new Shippenville plant and additional variations of the Fruit series appear in Chapter 3.

The early pieces pictured in this chapter are very rare and highly sought after by collectors, not only because of their rarity, but for their distinctive charm and simplicity.

A brochure printed by the Purinton Pottery Company of Wellsville, Ohio, describing the Peasant Ware line. It illustrates an advertising campaign promoted by *The New Yorker* magazine in the late 1930's.

Purinton Pottery

Purinton Pottery is a return to the feeling of the native crafts

For a long time there has been a strong demand in this country for primitive pottery. This has only been partially satisfied by importations from abroad. Purinton Pottery has been created to fill this need.

The clays used are native to this country and have been selected for their strength and color tone. The decorations follow closely those of native craftsmen, and are applied by an identical procedure—from an imaginative mind, by a skilled hand through the free brush to the molded clay. There can be no second guesses—when a stroke is made, it stays, or the piece is destroyed.

Purinton ware is the answer to what the style-conscious woman of today wants, to give a note of informal color to a room or table—either at parties or within the family circle. Its wide acceptance and undisputed vogue make it a profitable item for china and glass departments—and for gift departments too.

Write for further information to

PURINTON POTTERY
WELLSVILLE, OHIO

A brochure printed by the Purinton Pottery Company of Wellsville, Ohio, describing the PEASANT WARE line. It illustrates an advertising campaign promoted by *The New Yorker* magazine in the late 1930's.

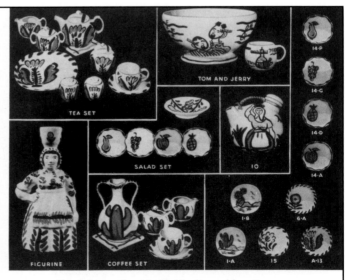

Above is shown a wide variety of Purinton shapes and decorations. These can be grouped in sets—tea sets, coffee sets, etc. The numbers shown are the numbers of the patterns, below are indicated the color combinations of some of the patterns.

1-A	Brown, Turquoise, Burnt Orange	14-A	Brown, Rose, Turquoise
1-B	Brown, Turquoise, Burnt Orange	14-G	Brown, Blue, Turquoise
6-A	Brown, Yellow, Turquoise	14-P	Brown, Yellow, Turquoise
A-13	Brown, Yellow, Turquoise	14-D	Brown, Burnt Orange, Turquoise

Purinton Pottery CO.
WELLSVILLE, OHIO

24

The Peasant Lady Candle-holders in the next four photos are extremely rare and highly sought after by collectors. They were originally sold in pairs and can be found in various colors and designs. The red, yellow, and teal versions seem to be the most common color combination. They all measure 10" in height. Many of them were hand signed on the bottom by William H. Blair.

PEASANT LADY Candleholders, pair
signed $1,000.00+
unsigned $800.00+

PEASANT LADY Candleholder, cobalt
unsigned each $500.00+

PEASANT LADY Candleholder
unsigned each $400.00+

PEASANT LADY Candleholder
signed each $500.00+

26

PEASANT GARDEN Breakfast Plate
8½" diameter
$100.00

PEASANT GARDEN Tea and Toast
Lap Plate, 8½" diameter, $90.00
Cup, 2½" high, $35.00

PEASANT GARDEN Chop Plate
12" diameter
$150.00

PEASANT GARDEN Open Vegetable
8½" diameter
$80.00

**PEASANT GARDEN Miniature
Jug-style Salt and Pepper
2½" high, pair $65.00**

**PEASANT GARDEN
Covered Sugar, 5" high
Creamer 3½" high
set $125.00**

**PEASANT GARDEN Pitcher
Rubel mold, 5" high
$125.00**

CACTUS FLOWER Fruit Bowl
12" diameter
$85.00

SUNFLOWER Tumbler
12 oz., 5" high
$30.00

SUNFLOWER Oasis Jug
9½" high, 9½" diameter
$500.00+

SUNFLOWER Breakfast Plate
8½" diameter
$45.00

DESERT SCENE Plate
8½" diameter
$75.00

DESERT SCENE Oasis Jug
9½" high, 9½" diameter
$500.00+

DESERT SCENE Plates
8½" diameter
(Hand signed "Purinton
Pottery.")
each $75.00

RIBBON FLOWER Oasis Jug
9½" high, 9½" diameter
$500.00+

RIBBON FLOWER 2-cup Teapot
Lid missing, 4" high
$50.00

RIBBON FLOWER Fruit Bowl
12" diameter
$50.00

DESERT FLOWER
Seahorse Cocktail
Dish
11¾" long
$55.00

FRUIT Seahorse
Cocktail Dish
11¾" long
$55.00

SOLID GLAZE Seahorse
Cocktail Dish
11¾" long
$35.00

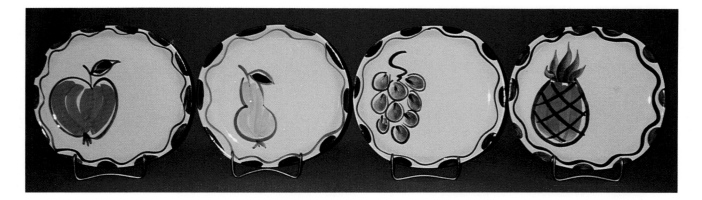

FRUIT Breakfast Plates (sold in luncheon sets)
8½" diameter
each $30.00

FRUIT Covered Sugar,
4" high
Creamer, 3" high
set $55.00

FRUIT Lap Plates
(to be used with cups)
8½" diameter
each $30.00

FRUIT Chop Plate
12" diameter
$35.00

Chapter 3

✥ Fruit Series ✥

Although the concept of using fruit designs began in the early years in Wellsville, Ohio, under the trade name of Peasant Ware, it eventually became a full line of ware sold as luncheon sets, tea and coffee sets, range sets, canisters, and other accessories. Production of this line probably began after the transition to Shippenville, Pennsylvania, and there are several variations. In one variation, probably the initial attempt, a red apple appears on the front of the piece and a yellow pear on the back, both outlined in dark brown. [See Figure 1.]

Figure 1: This photograph shows the front of a FRUIT 8-cup coffee pot depicting the apple motif and the back of a FRUIT 6-cup teapot depicting the pear motif.

In the case of the miniature salt, pepper, creamer, and sugar, one of the fruits would appear on each piece. Another, probably later, variation of the Fruit used an overlapping apple and pear motif. [See Figure 2.] Decorators also experimented with red and cobalt blue trim on the ware in addition to the design.

As the Purinton Company began to do private mold production for Esmond Industries of New York using the fruit scheme, this pattern took on other variations. The grape and pineapple motifs were used more commonly and the patterns became more detailed. In some instances the open apple of Chapter 4 was used instead of the solid apple used previously. Examples of these later variations appear on pages 48 – 51 and will

Figure 2: This FRUIT Flour Canister is a beautiful example of the overlapping apple-pear variation.

Figure 3: This later variation, named PROVIN-CIAL FRUIT, was not produced until 1955.

also be referred to as Fruit. The Fruit variations were heavily produced throughout the 1940's and well into the next decade, making these pieces readily available to collectors today.

In 1955 the Provincial Fruit design was introduced at the Pittsburgh Glass and Pottery Exhibit. [See Figure 3.] An advertisement from the April, 1955 *Crockery and Glass Journal* introducing this line appears on page 38. Although the advertisement labels this pattern as Fruit, the plant referred to this pattern as Provincial Fruit to differentiate from the previous fruit variations. Photographs in this chapter will adhere to the Provincial Fruit name in its identification of the ware. Few pieces of this variation can be found today as it was very limited in production.

Fruit

A BEST SELLER
AT THE PITTSBURGH SHOW

And with every reason to be! Purinton Ware, in open stock, is a moderate priced, oven proof, handcrafted product available in a variety of today's most popular color combinations. Each piece is individually decorated with free hand brush strokes and the decoration is absolutely permanent. Purinton, from the oven to the table to the automatic dishwasher without a care! Get your share of profits with this casual, modern ware . . . call, write or wire today.

PURINTON POTTERY CO.
SHIPPENVILLE, PENNSYLVANIA

CROCKERY & GLASS JOURNAL for April, 1955

An advertisement placed by the Purinton Pottery Co. in the April, 1955 issue of the *Crockery & Glass Journal.*

FRUIT
2-cup Individual Teapot, 4" high, $45.00
4-cup Teapot, 5" high, $55.00
6-cup Teapot, 6" high, $55.00

FRUIT
8-cup Coffee Pot, 8" high, $65.00
Covered Sugar, 4" high, $25.00
Creamer, 3" high, $15.00

FRUIT
6-cup Teapot with Drip Filter, 9" high, $75.00
8-cup Coffee Pot with Drip Filter, 11" high, $85.00

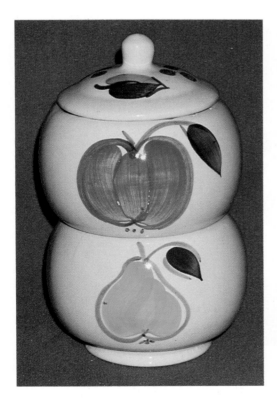

FRUIT Stacking Storage Jar
8¾" high, $85.00

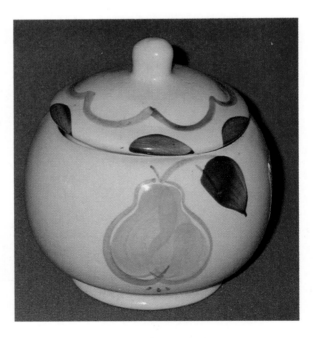

FRUIT Grease Jar
5½" high, $45.00

FRUIT Dinner Plate
9¾" diameter, $20.00
Complementary Cup & Saucer
(No FRUIT design)
Cup, 2½" high, $10.00
Saucer, 5½" diameter, $3.00

FRUIT Night Bottle and Tumbler
(Tumbler could be turned upside down on
top of bottle for storage on nightstand.)
Night Bottle, 1 quart, 7½" high, $45.00
Tumbler, 12 oz., 5" high, $20.00

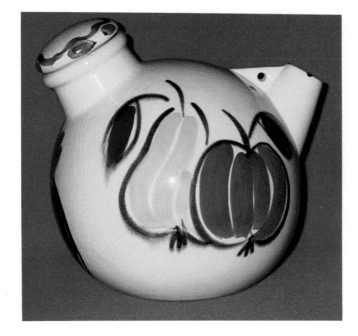

FRUIT Oasis Jug
9½" high, 9½" diameter
$500.00+

41

FRUIT
Dutch Jug, 2-pint, 5¾" high, $45.00
Jug, 5-pint, 8" high, $75.00

FRUIT
Juice Mug, 6 oz., 2½" high, $15.00
Tumbler 12 oz., 5" high, $20.00

FRUIT Oval-shaped Canister Set (Cobalt Trim)
9" high, each $65.00

FRUIT Vinegar Bottle
(Cobalt Trim)
1 pint, 9½" high
$35.00

FRUIT Oval-shaped Canisters (Red Trim)
9" high, each $60.00

FRUIT Oval-shaped Cookie Jar
(Red Trim)
9" high, $60.00

FRUIT Covered Range Bowls
(Red Trim)
5½" high, each $45.00

FRUIT Range-style Salt & Pepper
(Red Trim)
4" high, pair $40.00

FRUIT Square-shaped Oil and Vinegar Cruets (Solid apple/purple grapes) 5" high, $50.00

FRUIT Square-shaped Oil and Vinegar Cruets (Open apple/green grapes) 5" high, $55.00

FRUIT Covered Sugar and Creamer (Unusual mold) Sugar 4¼" high Creamer 3" high set $55.00

FRUIT Three-Section Relish
(Wood handle, solid apple/purple grapes)
10" diameter, $45.00

FRUIT Three-Section Relish
(Metal handle, open apple/green grapes)
10" diameter, $45.00

FRUIT Three-Section
Relish
(Pottery handle, earlier
variation of FRUITS)
10" diameter, $55.00

49

FRUIT Round Canisters (Wooden Lids)
7½" high
each $65.00

FRUIT Round Cookie Jar (Wooden Lid)
8" high
$70.00

PINEAPPLE Pickle Dish
(Unusual sponged edge)
6" diameter, $35.00

FRUIT Bean Pot on Warming Stand
Bean Pot 5¾" high, 9" high with stand
$65.00

GRAPES Bowl (Unusual mold)
4½" high, 5½" diameter
$45.00

GRAPES Covered Range Bowl
5½" high
$45.00

PROVINCIAL FRUIT
Meat Platter, 11" diameter, $40.00
Dinner Plate, 9¾" diameter, $20.00
Salad Plate, 6¾" diameter, $10.00
Cup, 2½" high, $10.00
Saucer, 5½" diameter, $3.00
Cereal Bowl, 5¼" diameter, $10.00

PROVINCIAL FRUIT
Fruit Bowl
12" diameter
$40.00

PROVINCIAL FRUIT Vase or Grease Jar
5" high, $30.00

PROVINCIAL FRUIT
Tumbler
12 oz., 5" high, $20.00

PROVINCIAL FRUIT
Stacking Salt & Pepper
2¼" high, pair $25.00

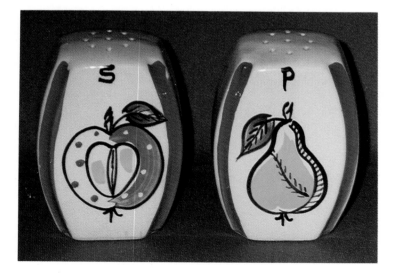

PROVINCIAL FRUIT
Range-style Salt & Pepper
4" high, pair $45.00

PROVINCIAL FRUIT
Three-Section Relish
10" diameter
$55.00

PROVINCIAL FRUIT
Covered Dish
9" long
$65.00

PROVINCIAL FRUIT
Bean Pot on Warming Stand
Bean Pot, 5¾" high, 9" with stand
set $65.00

54

Chapter 4

❦ Apple Series ❦

Purinton's hand-decorated ware had met with instant success with the production of the Fruit variations. They immediately set out to offer a full dinnerware line, and in the early 1940's William Blair designed the all-time favorite Apple pattern. Not only was this colorful pattern the best seller of the Purinton's for years to come, but it is by far the most sought after by collectors today.

Totally different from the apple motif of the Fruit variations, this new Apple pattern featured a ruby-red "open" apple with shades of yellow and brown inside, stems and leaves outlined and accented with dark brown, and two-tone leaves in shades of green and teal. Various trim colors in shades of teal, ruby-red, or cobalt were used on some pieces.

The initial offering of this line contained over 50 different open stock pieces. The pottery could be purchased as a six-piece place setting (for $4.95), a 16-piece starter set or service for four (for $10.95), a 32-piece dinner set or service for six (for $24.95), or a 53-piece dinner set or service for eight (for $39.95). A wide range of unique accessory pieces were offered in addition to the place settings.

This chapter illustrates all pieces that were offered in open stock with the addition of a few rare and unusual pieces that could be experimental in nature.

The beauty of the APPLE series is
breathtaking whether displayed as
a collection or set on a dinner table.

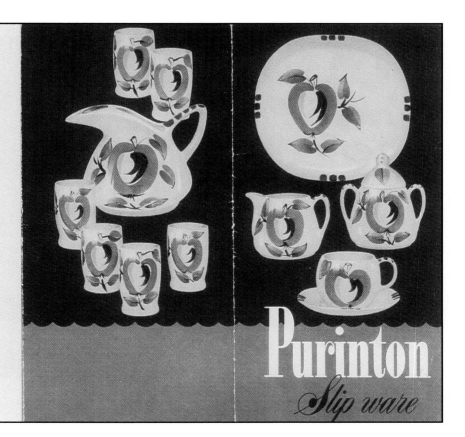

This brochure distributed by the Purinton Pottery Company in the 1940's provides a valuable reference for APPLE open stock items.

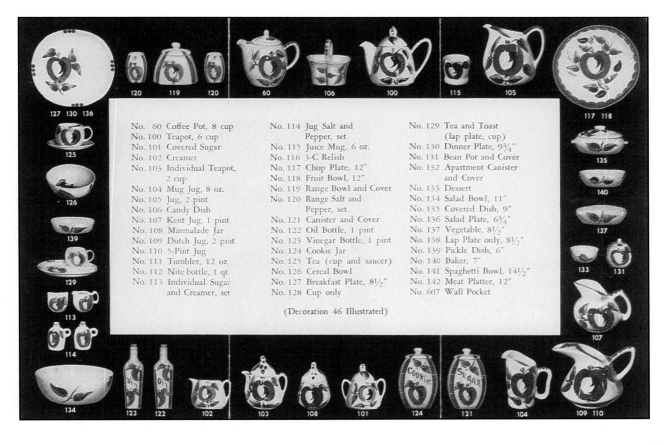

No. 60 Coffee Pot, 8 cup
No. 100 Teapot, 6 cup
No. 101 Covered Sugar
No. 102 Creamer
No. 103 Individual Teapot, 2 cup
No. 104 Mug Jug, 8 oz.
No. 105 Jug, 2 pint
No. 106 Candy Dish
No. 107 Kent Jug, 1 pint
No. 108 Marmalade Jar
No. 109 Dutch Jug, 2 pint
No. 110 5-Pint Jug
No. 111 Tumbler, 12 oz.
No. 112 Nite bottle, 1 qt
No. 113 Individual Sugar and Creamer, set

No. 114 Jug Salt and Pepper, set
No. 115 Juice Mug, 6 oz.
No. 116 3-C Relish
No. 117 Chop Plate, 12"
No. 118 Fruit Bowl, 12"
No. 119 Range Bowl and Cover
No. 120 Range Salt and Pepper, set
No. 121 Canister and Cover
No. 122 Oil Bottle, 1 pint
No. 123 Vinegar Bottle, 1 pint
No. 124 Cookie Jar
No. 125 Tea (cup and saucer)
No. 126 Cereal Bowl
No. 127 Breakfast Plate, 8½"
No. 128 Cup only

No. 129 Tea and Toast (lap plate, cup)
No. 130 Dinner Plate, 9¾"
No. 131 Bean Pot and Cover
No. 132 Apartment Canister and Cover
No. 133 Dessert
No. 134 Salad Bowl, 11"
No. 135 Covered Dish, 9"
No. 136 Salad Plate, 6¾"
No. 137 Vegetable, 8½"
No. 138 Lap Plate only, 8½"
No. 139 Pickle Dish, 6"
No. 140 Baker, 7"
No. 141 Spaghetti Bowl, 14½"
No. 142 Meat Platter, 12"
No. 607 Wall Pocket

(Decoration 46 Illustrated)

APPLE
Dinner Plate, 9¾" diameter, $15.00
Breakfast Plate, 8½" diameter, $12.00
Salad Plate, 6¾" diameter, $10.00
Cereal Bowl, 5¼" diameter, $10.00
Dessert Bowl, 4" diameter, $8.00
Cup, 2½" high, $10.00
Saucer, 5½" diameter, $3.00

APPLE Tea and Toast
Lap Plate, 8½" diameter, $15.00
Cup, 2½" high, $10.00

APPLE Meat Platter
12" diameter, $40.00

APPLE Grill Platters
(Note indentations on surface.)
12" diameter, each $45.00

APPLE Oval Platter
(This rare platter was not an open stock mold.)
14" diameter, $50.00

APPLE Chop Plate
(Scalloped Border)
12" diameter, $40.00

APPLE Chop Plate
(Plain Border)
12" diameter, $35.00

APPLE Fruit Bowl
\ **(Plain Border)**
12" diameter, $35.00

APPLE Fruit Bowl
(Scalloped Border)
12" diameter, $40.00

APPLE Divided Vegetable
10½" long, $35.00

APPLE Roll Tray
11" long, $35.00

APPLE Covered Dish
9" long, $65.00

APPLE Open Vegetable
8½" diameter, $25.00

APPLE Salad Bowl
11" diameter
$50.00

APPLE Baker
7" diameter
$30.00

APPLE Butter Dish
6½" long
$65.00

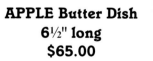

APPLE Jam & Jelly Dish
5½" long
$45.00

APPLE Pickle Dish
6" diameter
$30.00

APPLE Three-Section Relish
10" diameter
$55.00

APPLE
Marmalade Jar, 4½" high, $50.00
Bean Pot, 3¾" high, $50.00

APPLE
Covered Sugar, 5" high, $30.00
Creamer, 3½" high, $20.00
(Note: The APPLE creamer was also sold with a lid as an individual teapot. See page 69.)

APPLE
Beverage Pitcher
2 pint, 6¼" high, $65.00
Dutch Jug
2 pint, 5¾" high, $55.00
Jug
5 pint, 8" high, $85.00

APPLE
Juice Mug
6 oz., 2½" high, $15.00
Tumbler
12 oz., 5" high, $20.00

APPLE
Handled Mug
8 oz., 4" high, $35.00
Mug Jug
8 oz., 4¾" high, $55.00
Beer Mug
16 oz., 4¾" high, $55.00

APPLE Honey Jug
6¼" high
$55.00

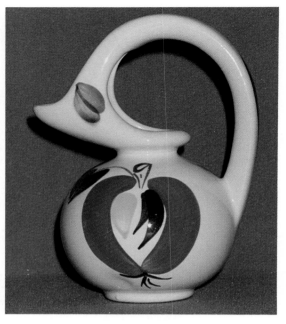

APPLE Night Bottle and Tumbler
(Tumbler could be turned
upside down on top of bottle for
storage on nightstand.)
Tumbler, 12 oz., 5" high, $20.00
Night Bottle, 1 quart, 7½" high, $55.00

APPLE
Kent-Style Jug
(Rare size)
6¼" high, $65.00
Kent Jug
1 pint, 4½" high, $35.00

APPLE
2-Cup Teapot
(Purinton's creamer could double as a teapot
using a lid similar to that on the sugar bowl.)
5" high, $40.00
6-Cup Teapot
6½" high, $70.00

APPLE 8-Cup Coffee Pot
8" high
$90.00

APPLE 8-Cup Coffee Pot with Drip Filter
11" high
$110.00

APPLE Tall Oil and Vinegar Bottles
1 pint, 9½" high
pair $95.00

APPLE Square-shaped
Oil and Vinegar Cruets
5" high
pair $75.00

APPLE Covered Grease Jar
5½" high
$85.00

**APPLE
Pour 'N Shake
Shakers
4¼" high
each $40.00**

APPLE
Covered Range Bowl
5½" high, $65.00
Range-style
Salt & Pepper
4" high, pair $50.00

APPLE Stacking Salt & Pepper
2¼" high
pair $35.00

APPLE
Miniature Jug-style
Salt & Pepper
2½" high
pair $20.00
Miniature
Creamer and
Sugar Set
2" high
set $30.00
(Made for "break-
fast in bed.")

73

APPLE Oval-shaped Canister Set (Red Trim)
9" high, each $60.00

APPLE Oval-shaped Canister Set (Rare Cobalt Trim)
9" high, each $75.00

APPLE Round Canister Set (Rare set with wooden lids)
Flour and Sugar, 8" high, Coffee and Tea, 7½" high, each $75.00

APPLE Square Canister Set
Flour and Coffee, 7½" high
Sugar and Tea, 5½" high
each $50.00

APPLE Half-Oval Canister Set
5½" high
each $65.00

APPLE Oval-shaped Cookie Jars
(Jar on right is same mold as oval-shaped canisters.)
9½" high (on left), $75.00
9" high, $60.00

APPLE Square-shaped Cookie Jar
with Wooden Lid
9½" high
$90.00

APPLE Candy Dish
6¼" high
$50.00

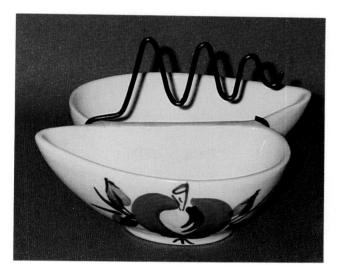

APPLE Ashtray
5½" long
$40.00

APPLE Candleholders
6" diameter, 2" high
each $45.00

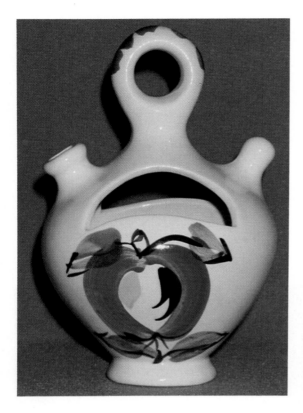

APPLE Rum Jug Planter
6½" high
$55.00

APPLE Wall Pocket
3½" high
$40.00

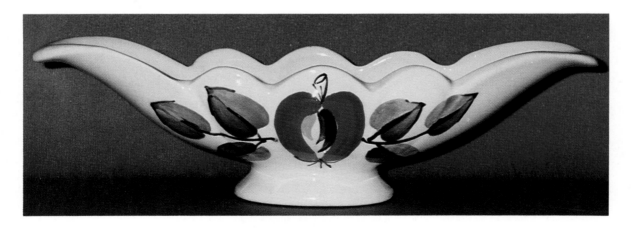

APPLE Console Bowl (NAPCO mold)
11" long, $75.00

APPLE Bean Pot on Warming Stand
Bean Pot, 5¾" high
9" high including stand (not including handle)
$65.00

APPLE Pitcher (Rubel mold)
5" high
$75.00

APPLE Lazy Susan
(Rare mold —
middle section is
relish tray on page 65.)
16" diameter
$125.00

APPLE Individualized Dinner Plate
(Hand signed by Dorothy Purinton.)
9¾" diameter
signed $225.00+

APPLE Experimental Dish
7½" diameter
$45.00

APPLE Candy Dish
(Rare mold)
5¾" diameter
$75.00

80

Chapter 5

❦ Intaglio Series ❧

Perhaps the small Pennsylvania community of Shippenville, nestled in the foothills of the Allegheny Mountains, inspired the quaint Intaglio pattern. Its rich brown color and woodsy designs are reminiscent of a wooded countryside.

William Blair was the first to experiment with the Intaglio concept of incising a design into a background of brush-stroked color. Some of his rare artwork in the Intaglio style is illustrated in Chapter 12. However, Dorothy Purinton is credited with the design of the main Intaglio line which featured a mountain flower and leaf design incised into a background of deep brown strokes of color. This new pattern was introduced in June, 1950 in a promotion through Bigelow's Department Store, one of the leading department stores in the state of New York at that time.

Although the brown Intaglio was heavily produced, a more limited production of the same design on a blue-green background was produced in the mid-1950's. This pattern was called Turquoise, examples of which appear in this chapter.

Other designs can be found in the Intaglio style on various colors of brush-stroked background, such as the elusive Palm Tree designs on colors of royal blue, coral red, and purple. A leaf design was incised into a carmel-colored background. These pieces are rare and were not offered in a regular line, hence, photographs identifying these unique examples appear in Chapter 12. However, it should be noted that the Purinton Company's reference to Intaglio meant the brown-colored version with the mountain flower and/or leaf motif which is illustrated in this chapter.

An ad from the Jamestown (NY) *Post-Journal* on June 7, 1950 featuring Bigelow's promotion of Purinton Pottery. The featured patterns were APPLE, INTAGLIO, and MAYWOOD.

The wide variety offered in the INTAGLIO series makes it a desirable collectible for use as a dinnerware setting. Its rich brown color adds warmth to the country atmosphere in this room.

INTAGLIO
Dinner Plate, 9¾" diameter, $15.00
Breakfast Plate, 8½" diameter, $10.00
Salad Plate, 6¾" diameter, $10.00
Cereal Bowl, 5¼" diameter, $10.00
Dessert Bowl, 4" diameter, $8.00
Cup, 2½" high, $10.00
Saucer, 5½" diameter, $3.00

INTAGLIO Tea and Toast
Lap Plate, 8½" diameter, $15.00
Cup, 2½" high, $10.00

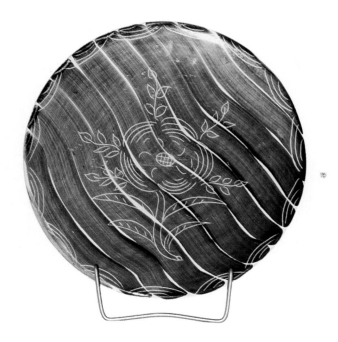

INTAGLIO Chop Plate
12" diameter
$25.00

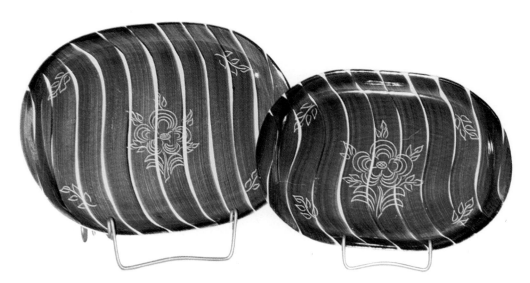

INTAGLIO Meat Platters
12" diameter (left), 11" diameter (right)
each $30.00

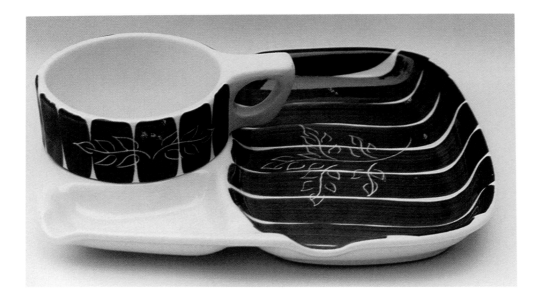

INTAGLIO Soup and Sandwich (Rubel mold)
Plate, 11" diameter
Cup, 2¼" high, 4" diameter
set $50.00

INTAGLIO Gravy Pitcher (TS&T mold)
3¾" high
$65.00

INTAGLIO Divided Vegetable
10½" long
$30.00

INTAGLIO Roll Tray
11" long
$35.00

INTAGLIO Baker
7" diameter
$20.00

INTAGLIO Open Vegetable
8½" diameter
$20.00

INTAGLIO Jam & Jelly Dish
5½" long
$40.00

INTAGLIO Butter Dish
6½" long
$55.00

INTAGLIO Candy Dish
(NAPCO mold — note
unusual PENNSYLVA-
NIA DUTCH design.)
6" long
$35.00

INTAGLIO Covered Range Bowl
5½" high
$45.00

INTAGLIO Bean Pot
3¾" high
$50.00

INTAGLIO Covered Dish
9" long
$55.00

INTAGLIO Tidbit Tray
10" diameter
$55.00

INTAGLIO Three-Section Relish
(Metal handle)
10" diameter
$45.00

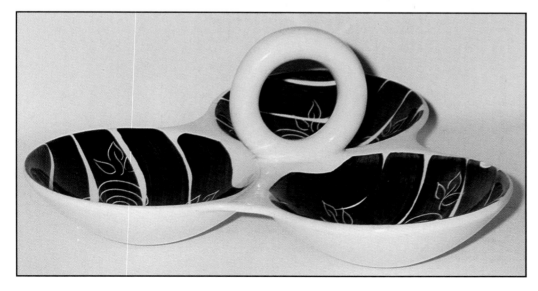

INTAGLIO
Three-Section Relish
(Pottery handle)
10" diameter
$45.00

**INTAGLIO Coffee Server
(This was a mold used for
the SEAFORM pattern.)
9" high
$100.00**

**INTAGLIO
Covered Sugar, 5" high, $30.00
Creamer, 3½" high, $20.00**

**INTAGLIO Pour 'N Shake
Salt and Pepper
4¼" high
pair $50.00**

**INTAGLIO Miniature Jug-style
Salt and Pepper
2½" high
pair $20.00**

**INTAGLIO Miniature Decanter
5" high
$35.00**

INTAGLIO Oval-shaped Cookie Jar
9½" high
$75.00

INTAGLIO Square-shaped Cookie Jar
with Wooden Lid
9½" high
$75.00

INTAGLIO 6-cup Teapot
6½" high
$65.00

INTAGLIO Jug
5 pint, 8" high
$75.00

INTAGLIO
Pitcher (Rubel mold), 5" high, $55.00
Beverage Pitcher, 2 pint, 6¼" high, $55.00

INTAGLIO
Kent Jug
1 pint, 4½" high
$30.00
Mug Jug
8 oz., 4¾" high
$40.00

INTAGLIO
Handled Mug
8 oz., 4" high, $25.00
Beer Mug
16 oz., 4¾" high, $40.00

INTAGLIO
Juice Mug
(Unusual grape design)
6 oz., 2½" high, $20.00
Tumbler
12 oz., 5" high, $20.00
Mug (Unusual mold)
5" high, $50.00

TURQUOISE
Dinner Plate, 9¾" diameter, $15.00
Salad Plate, 6¾" diameter, $10.00
Dessert Bowl, 4" diameter, $8.00
Cup, 2½" high, $10.00
Saucer, 5½" diameter, $3.00

TURQUOISE Soup and Sandwich (Rubel mold)
Plate, 11" diameter
Cup, 2¼" high, 4" diameter
$55.00

TURQUOISE Kent Jug
1 pint, 4½" high
$40.00

TURQUOISE Miniature
Jug-style Salt and Pepper
2½" high
pair $30.00

TURQUOISE Stacking
Salt Shaker
2¼" high
pair $30.00

TURQUOISE Baker
7" diameter
$30.00

TURQUOISE Divided Vegetable
10½" long
$35.00

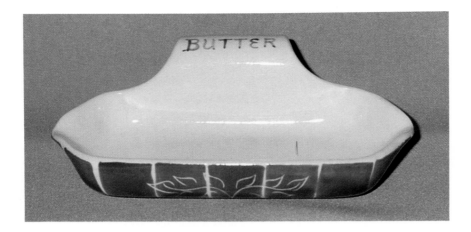

TURQUOISE Butter Dish
6½" long
$75.00

TURQUOISE Fruit Bowl
12" diameter
$40.00

Chapter 6

❧ Heather Plaid Series ❧

This delightful line of dinnerware designed by William Blair made its debut as a "sister" pattern to Normandy Plaid at the Pittsburgh Glass and Pottery Exhibit in December of 1951. The plaid, predominantly teal green with red and yellow accents, makes a striking contrast on Purinton's cream-colored slip making these pieces hard to resist. The Heather Plaid production volume was significantly lower than the Normandy version even though pieces were offered in open stock. Dinnerware items, especially accessory pieces, are difficult to find.

HEATHER PLAID
Dinner Plate, 9¾" diameter, $15.00
Salad Plate, 6¾" diameter, $10.00
Dessert Bowl, 4" diameter, $8.00
Cup, 2½" high, $10.00
Saucer, 5½" diameter, $3.00

HEATHER PLAID Tea and Toast
Lap Plate, 8½" diameter, $15.00
Cup, 2½" high, $10.00

HEATHER PLAID Chop Plate
12" diameter
$25.00

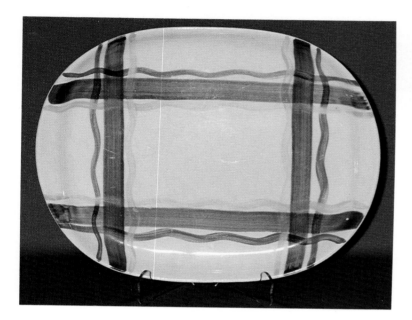

HEATHER PLAID Meat Platter
12" diameter
$30.00

HEATHER PLAID Open Vegetable
8½" diameter
$20.00

HEATHER PLAID
Divided Vegetable
10½" long
$30.00

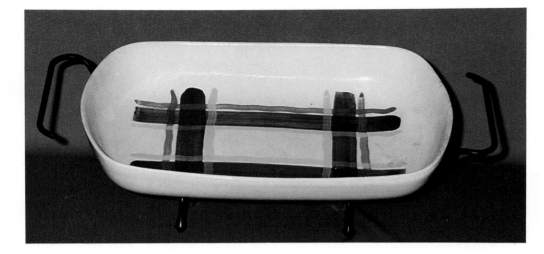

HEATHER PLAID
Roll Tray on Stand
Tray, 11" long
Stand, 14" long
$35.00

HEATHER PLAID
Oval-shaped Cookie Jar
9½" high
$60.00

HEATHER PLAID
Square Coffee Canister
7½" high
$40.00

HEATHER PLAID
Covered Grease jar
5½" high
$60.00

HEATHER PLAID
Pour 'N Shake
Salt and Pepper
4¼" high
pair $60.00

HEATHER PLAID
Miniature Jug-style Salt and Pepper
2½" high
pair $20.00

HEATHER PLAID
Dutch Jug (left), 2 pint, 5¾" high, $45.00
Jug, 5 pint, 8" high, $75.00

HEATHER PLAID 6-cup Teapot
6" high
$65.00

HEATHER PLAID
Kent Jug
1 pint, 4½" high
$30.00

HEATHER PLAID
Handled Mug
8 oz., 4" high
$25.00

HEATHER PLAID
Creamer
3" high, $20.00
Covered Sugar
4" high, $30.00

HEATHER PLAID
Jam and Jelly Dish
5½" long
$35.00

HEATHER PLAID
Wall Pocket
3½" high
$35.00

HEATHER PLAID
Rum Jug Planter
6½" high
$40.00

Chapter 7

❧ Normandy Plaid Series ❧

The Purinton Pottery Company described their new Normandy Plaid pattern as "pert, saucy... but beautiful," and after over 40 years it is still an accurate description of this colorful series. Designed by William Blair, the plaid was predominantly ruby-red with accents of chartreuse and forest green hand-painted on the creamy-white body. It was originally offered in a 16-piece starter set with 41 pieces in open stock. Many examples of these pieces are illustrated in this chapter as a general guide for the collector.

With its warmth and charm, Normandy Plaid blends well with today's popular color schemes of red and green and has become a favorite among pottery collectors.

A brochure distributed by the Purinton Pottery Company listing the open stock pieces available in the NORMANDY PLAID pattern.

"Normandy Plaid" in Open Stock

No.	Item	No.	Item
60	Coffee Pot, 8 cup	133	Dessert
104	Mug Jug, 8 oz.	135	Covered Dish, 9"
105	Jug, 2 pint	136	Salad Plate, 6¾"
106	Candy Dish	137	Vegetable, 8"
107	Kent Jug (Sauce Pitcher), 1 pt.	139	Pickle Dish, 6"
108	Marmalade Jar	140	Baker, 7"
109	Dutch Jug, 2 pint	141	Spaghetti Bowl, 14½"
110	5-Pint Jug	142	Meat Platter, 12"
111	Tumbler, 12 oz.	143	Cookie Jar
114	Jug Salt & Pepper Set	145	Handled Mug
115	Juice Mug, 6 oz.	146	Beer Mug
116	3-C Relish Dish	148	Range Salt & Pepper Set
117	Chop Plate, 12"	149	Range Bowl & Cover
118	Fruit Bowl, 12"	150	Canister & Cover
125	Tea (cup & saucer)	151	Oil & Vinegar Jugs
126	Cereal Bowl	202	Covered Sugar
127	Breakfast Plate, 8½"	204	Creamer
129	Tea & Toast (lap plate, cup)	404	Teapot, 6 cup
130	Dinner Plate, 9¾"		

"Normandy Plaid"

SLIP WARE

by

Purinton

P ERT, saucy . . . but beautiful! For the most unusual in table settings, select PURINTON'S exciting new pattern, "Normandy Plaid". Sixteen-piece Starter Set, and forty-one other pieces in Open Stock.

PURINTON POTTERY COMPANY
Shippenville, Pennsylvania
"Creators of America's Most Unusual Dinnerware"

NORMANDY PLAID
Dinner Plate (left)
9¾" diameter
$15.00
Chop Plate
12" diameter
$25.00

NORMANDY PLAID
Dessert Bowl (left), 4" diameter, $8.00
Cereal Bowl, 5¼" diameter, $10.00

NORMANDY PLAID
Cup, 2½" high, $10.00
Saucer, 5½" diameter, $3.00

NORMANDY PLAID
Tea and Toast
Lap Plate, 8½" diameter, $15.00
Cup, 2½" high, $10.00

NORMANDY PLAID
Meat Platter
12" diameter
$30.00

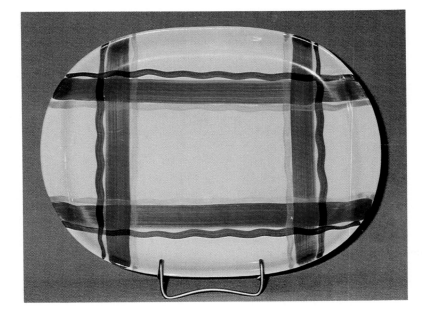

NORMANDY PLAID
Fruit Bowl
12" diameter
$35.00

NORMANDY PLAID
Open Vegetable
8½" diameter
$20.00

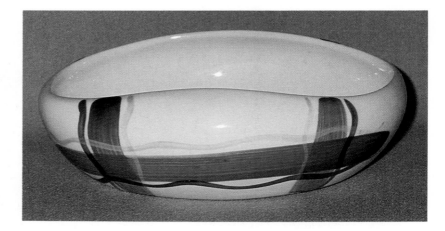

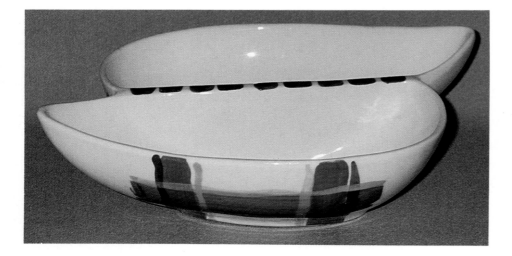

NORMANDY PLAID
Divided Vegetable
10½" long
$30.00

NORMANDY PLAID Spaghetti Bowl
14½" long, $55.00

NORMANDY PLAID Roll Tray
11" long, $35.00

NORMANDY PLAID
Oval-shaped Cookie Jar
9½" high
$60.00

NORMANDY PLAID
Bean Pot
3¾" high
$50.00

NORMANDY PLAID
Covered Range Bowl
5½" high
$50.00

NORMANDY PLAID
Covered Dish
9" long
$55.00

NORMANDY PLAID
Dutch Jug, 2 pint, 5¾" high, $45.00
Jug, 5 pint, 8" high, $75.00

NORMANDY PLAID
6-cup Teapot
6" high
$65.00

NORMANDY PLAID
Beverage Pitcher
2 pint, 6¼" high
$55.00

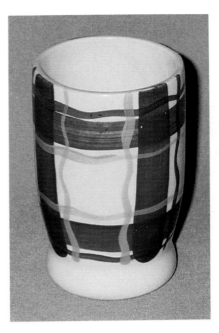

NORMANDY PLAID
Tumbler
12 oz., 5" high
$20.00

NORMANDY PLAID Beer Mug
16 oz., 4¾" high
$40.00

NORMANDY PLAID Handled Mug
8 oz., 4" high
$25.00

NORMANDY PLAID Coffee Mug
(Very unusual — probably experimental)
3" high
$65.00

NORMANDY PLAID
Mug Jug
8 oz., 4¾" high
$40.00

NORMANDY PLAID
Souvenir Mug
(Under-glaze decal from Penn. State)
16 oz., 4¾" high
$75.00

NORMANDY PLAID
Kent Jug
1 pint, 4½" high
$30.00

NORMANDY PLAID
Stacking Salt and Pepper
2¼" high
pair $25.00

NORMANDY PLAID
Miniature
Creamer and Sugar
2" high, set $30.00
Miniature Jug-style
Salt and Pepper
2½" high, pair $20.00

NORMANDY PLAID
Square-shaped Oil and Vinegar Cruets
5" high
pair $55.00

NORMANDY PLAID
Jug-style Oil and Vinegar Cruets
5" high
pair $65.00

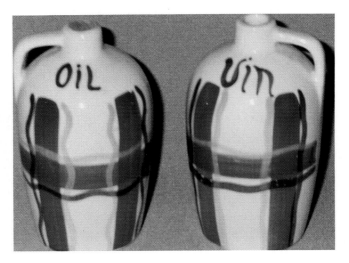

NORMANDY PLAID
Pour 'N Shake Shakers
4¼" high
each $30.00

NORMANDY PLAID
Pour 'N Shake Salt and Pepper
4¼" high
pair $60.00

NORMANDY PLAID
Covered Grease jar
5½" high
$60.00

NORMANDY PLAID
Candy Dish
6¼" high
$35.00

NORMANDY PLAID
Three-Section Relish
10" diameter
$45.00

NORMANDY PLAID Square Canister Set
Flour and Coffee 7½" high, Sugar and Tea 5½" high, each $40.00

Chapter 8

❧ Maywood Series ❧

Along with the introduction of the Intaglio series in 1950, the Purintons met with instant success on still another series. Bernard Purinton decided to name this beautiful pattern Maywood. It was unique in that it was dipped in a slip that eventually fired to a greenish-gray color, rather than Purinton's traditional creamy white body. It was rather perplexing at times to keep this line separate from the others as it was impossible to differentiate between the Maywood body and the regular cream body when the greenware was still wet. A brilliant white dogwood flower pattern, outlined in black, with a yellow center and tiny green leaves appears in the center of each piece.

The Maywood series was one of the patterns included in the large promotion of Purinton pottery at Bigelow's Department Store in Jamestown, New York in June, 1950. See page 82 in Chapter 5 for a copy of an ad describing the Maywood pattern as giving "warmth and dignity to your hospitality" and selling a starter set for four for $8.95. In this ad the miniature jug-style salt and pepper sets were offered free to June brides with the purchase of a starter set.

MAYWOOD
Dinner Plate, 9¾" diameter, $10.00
Salad Plate, 6¾" diameter, $8.00
Juice Mug, 6 oz., 2½" high, $15.00
Cup, 2½" high, $8.00
Saucer, 5½" diameter, $3.00
Dessert Bowl, 4" diameter, $6.00
Cereal Bowl, 5¼" diameter, $8.00

MAYWOOD
Chop Plate (left), 12" diameter, $20.00
Fruit Bowl, 12" diameter, $20.00

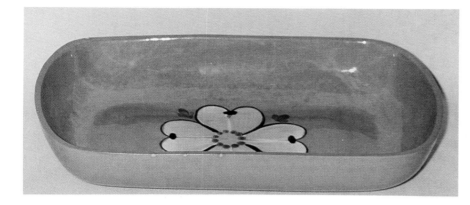

MAYWOOD Roll Tray
11" long
$20.00

MAYWOOD Salad Bowl
11" diameter
$25.00

MAYWOOD Grill Platter
12" diameter
$25.00

MAYWOOD Tea and Toast
Lap Plate, 8½" diameter, $10.00
Cup, 2½" high, $8.00

MAYWOOD Kent Jug
1 pint, 4½" high
$25.00

MAYWOOD Miniature Jug-style
Salt and Pepper
2½" high
$15.00

MAYWOOD
6-cup Teapot (left)
6½" high, $45.00
8-cup Coffee Pot
8" high, $65.00

MAYWOOD
Open Vegetable (left)
8½" diameter, $15.00
Covered Dish
9" long, $35.00

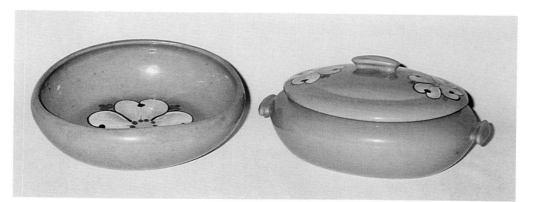

MAYWOOD
Baker (left)
7 " diameter, $15.00
Pickle Dish
6" diameter, $15.00

MAYWOOD
Three-Section Relish
10" diameter
$35.00

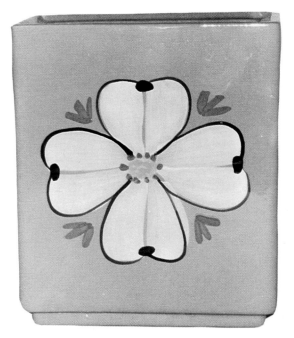

MAYWOOD Pillow Vase
6¾" high, $25.00
(This was a NAPCO mold which
Purinton used extensively for florist
ware and for the square canister sets.)

MAYWOOD 2-cup Teapot
5" high, $35.00
(This teapot bottom is the same mold
used for the creamer. Using a sugar bowl
lid, it was sold as an individual teapot.)

Chapter 9

✤ Saraband Series ✤

The Saraband pattern was fashioned in much the same manner as the Intaglio backgrounds with its gracefully swerving narrow bands of color. Shades of deep brown, chartreuse, and medium green carried on the woodsy color theme used on so much of Purinton's ware. This series was heavily produced in the dinnerware line, although accessory pieces seem to be more difficult to find. Although a continuously steady seller for the Purintons in the 1950's, Saraband's popularity in the collector's market is somewhat mediocre, probably due to its dated color scheme.

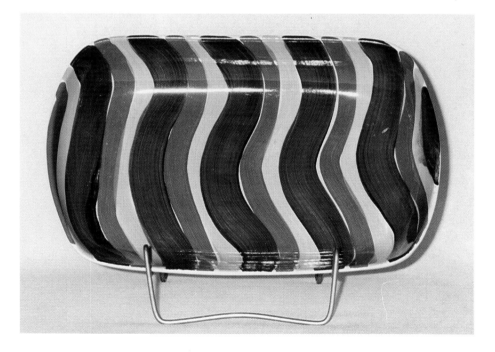

SARABAND
Dinner Plate, 9¾" diameter, $8.00
Salad Plate, 6¾" diameter, $4.00
Cereal Bowl, 5¼" diameter, $4.00
Cup, 2½" high, $5.00
Saucer, 5½" diameter, $2.00

SARABAND Tea and Toast
Lap Plate, 8½" diameter, $8.00
Cup, 2½" high, $5.00

SARABAND Fruit Bowl
12" diameter
$15.00

SARABAND Chop Plate
12" diameter
$15.00

SARABAND Roll Tray
11" long
$12.00

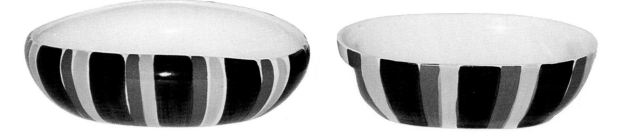

SARABAND
Open Vegetable, 8½" diameter, $10.00
Baker, 7" diameter, $10.00

SARABAND
Covered Dish
9" long
$25.00

SARABAND
Candleholder
6" diameter, 2" high
$20.00

SARABAND
Square Canister Set
(Sugar is missing)
Flour and Coffee, 7½" high
Sugar and Tea, 5½" high
each $25.00

SARABAND Tea Canister
(One section of a set of four which revolved upon a
wood base and were covered with a wooden lid.)
7" high
set $35.00

SARABAND Oval-shaped Cookie Jar
9½" high
$30.00

SARABAND Beer Mug
16 oz., 4¾" high
$15.00

SARABAND 6-cup Teapot
6½" high
$25.00

SARABAND Covered Range Bowl
5½" high
$20.00

SARABAND
Stacking Salt and Pepper
2¼" high
pair $10.00

SARABAND
Miniature Jug-style Salt and Pepper
2½" high
pair $10.00

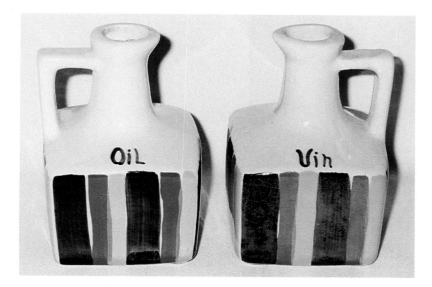

OiL   Vin

SARABAND
Square-shaped
Oil and Vinegar Cruets
5" high
pair $25.00

Chapter 10

❧ Pennsylvania Dutch Series ❧

Although most of Purinton's patterns were meant to portray a Pennsylvania Dutch theme, this series more than any other represents the true folk-art tradition of Pennsylvania's past. Several variations of this pattern will be found, not only in this chapter, but also with the more unusual items of Chapter 12. However, the basic pattern was used on a line of regular dinnerware items produced in open stock in the early 1950's. It featured the use of two traditional motifs, a heart and a stylized tulip, and their use depended on the particular piece being decorated. Both designs were basically a pinkish mauve with delicate accents of turquoise encircled with tiny leaves in shades of medium green and teal.

Production of this pattern was rather limited compared to other dinnerware lines, thus making pieces extremely difficult to find today. In addition to its rarity, the fact that collectors favor this pattern because of its homespun folk art appearance, make these examples of Purinton slip ware highly prized collectibles.

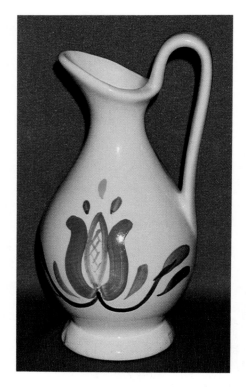

**Very early version of the PENNSYLVANIA DUTCH
pattern — probably an experimental line.
Dinner Plate, 9¾" diameter, $125.00**

**Two variations of the PENNSYLVANIA DUTCH pattern —
the plate on the left is probably an older style.
Dinner Plates, 9¾" diameter
Left, $35.00, right, $25.00**

PENNSYLVANIA DUTCH
Dinner Plate, 9¾" diameter, $25.00
Salad Plate, 6¾" diameter, $20.00
Cereal Bowl, 5¼" diameter, $20.00
Dessert Bowl, 4" diameter, $15.00
Cup, 2½" diameter, $20.00
Saucer, 5½" diameter, $8.00

PENNSYLVANIA DUTCH
Tea and Toast
Lap Plate, 8½" diameter
$35.00
Cup, 2½" high
$20.00

PENNSYLVANIA DUTCH Soup and Sandwich (Rubel mold)
Plate, 11" diameter
Cup, 2¼" high, 4" diameter
set $75.00

PENNSYLVANIA DUTCH Meat Platter
12" diameter
$50.00

PENNSYLVANIA DUTCH
Open Vegetable
8½" diameter
$40.00

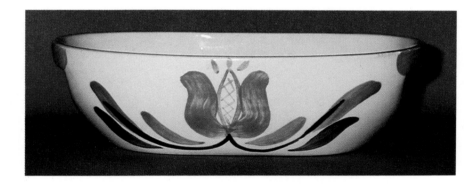

PENNSYLVANIA DUTCH
Baker
7" diameter
$45.00

PENNSYLVANIA DUTCH Divided Vegetable
10½" long, $50.00

PENNSYLVANIA DUTCH
Three-Section Relish
(Pottery Handle)
10" diameter
$75.00

PENNSYLVANIA DUTCH
Three-Section Relish
(Metal Handle)
10" diameter
$75.00

PENNSYLVANIA DUTCH Jam and Jelly Dishes
Unusual style with hole in handle (left), standard open stock mold (right)
Both 5½" long, each $65.00

PENNSYLVANIA DUTCH Dutch Jug
2 pint, 5¾" high
$100.00

PENNSYLVANIA DUTCH
Beer Mug
16 oz., 4¾" high
$65.00

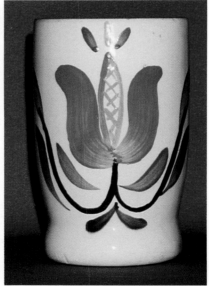

PENNSYLVANIA DUTCH
Tumbler
12 oz., 5" high
$35.00

PENNSYLVANIA DUTCH
Miniature Jug-style Salt and Pepper
2½" high
pair, $40.00

PENNSYLVANIA DUTCH
Pour 'N Shake Salt and Pepper
4¼" high
pair, $100.00

PENNSYLVANIA DUTCH
Stacking Salt and Pepper
2¼" high
pair, $50.00

PENNSYLVANIA DUTCH
Pour 'N Shake Shakers
4¼" high
each $50.00

PENNSYLVANIA DUTCH
Covered Sugar
5" high, $50.00
Creamer
3½" high, $40.00

PENNSYLVANIA DUTCH
Square-shaped Oil and Vinegar Cruets
5" high
pair $125.00

142

PENNSYLVANIA DUTCH
Slant-top Cookie Jar with Wooden Lid
7" high, 7" deep
$125.00

PENNSYLVANIA DUTCH
Square-shaped Cookie Jars
With wooden lid, 9½" high, $110.00
With pottery lid, 9½" high, $125.00

PENNSYLVANIA DUTCH Square-shaped Canister Set with Wooden Lids
Flour and Sugar, 9½" high
Coffee and Tea, 5½" high
each $85.00

PENNSYLVANIA DUTCH Square Canister Set
Flour and Coffee, 7½" high
Sugar and Tea, 5½" high
each $100.00

PENNSYLVANIA DUTCH
Basket Planter
6¼" high
$85.00

PENNSYLVANIA DUTCH Candy Dishes (NAPCO mold)
5" long (left), 6" long (right)
each $50.00

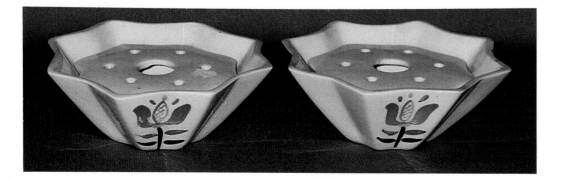

PENNSYLVANIA DUTCH Candleholders
6" diameter, 2" high
each $65.00

PENNSYLVANIA DUTCH
Pitcher (Unusual Rubel mold)
5" high
$100.00

PENNSYLVANIA DUTCH-STYLE
Pitcher
This is a very unusual example of a
Pennsylvania Dutch variation, probably
experimental in nature. This pitcher
mold is also very unusual and was not
offered in open stock.
7½" high
$125.00

PENNSYLVANIA DUTCH Candy Dish
6¼" high
$65.00

PENNSYLVANIA DUTCH Wall Pocket
3½" high
$65.00

PENNSYLVANIA DUTCH Honey Jug
6¼" high
$85.00

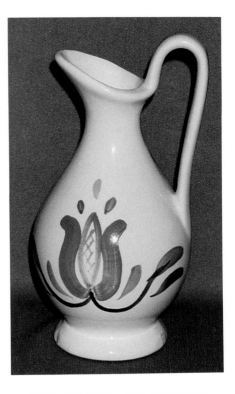

PENNSYLVANIA DUTCH
Rebecca Jug
7½" high
$75.00

Chapter 11

❧ Miscellaneous Slip Ware ❧

The dinnerware lines illustrated in Chapters 3 through 10 were produced in unlimited quantities and offered in open stock. Other dinnerware lines followed, namely the Crescent Flower, Seaform, Tea Rose, Mountain Rose, Petals, Chartreuse, and Ming Tree patterns, but were produced in limited number and are generally difficult to locate.

The Seaform series was actually named for its shape as well as the pattern applied to it. Its unique molds were not used for any other dinnerware series; however, individualized plates using this mold are illustrated in Chapter 12. Tea Rose is a lovely floral pattern but apparently was a slow seller and its line was soon discontinued. Mountain Rose is a striking pattern with its vivid colors and, although dinnerware pieces are rare, its 2-cup teapot was heavily produced for a contract with the McCormick Tea Company when the Tionesta plant opened. The Petals pattern was produced for sale by the Sears, Roebuck and Company and this colorful pattern is a favorite with collectors. Chartreuse, Crescent Flower, and the oriental-style Ming Tree series are fairly difficult to find.

The Purinton Company developed many other patterns that were used mainly on hollow ware, such as the Ivy and Daisy series. Ivy was heavily produced in tea sets and jugs and has variations in either a red or yellow blossom.

The elusive Palm Tree line was developed specifically for sale by a souvenir and gift shop in Florida owned by one of Bernard Purinton's sons. This rare and desirable pattern was offered in a variety of ware, some of which are illustrated in this chapter. For other rare variations of the Palm Tree pattern which were also sold in Florida, be sure to see Chapter 12.

Many specialty items, such as small vases and planters, were sold to gift and florist shops. They were decorated in a wide array of unnamed patterns and sold by the dozen to retailers. Containers were sold for assorted products such as toiletries, condiments, and liquors and used for premium sales. Many items were popularly referred to by their shape rather than pattern, such as the honey jug which was originally designed to sell honey. The two-cup teapot was a popular item used as a premium by tea companies.

The Purintons designed three figural cookie jars which were produced on a regular production line: the "Pig With Corn Cob," "Humpty Dumpty," and "Rooster," all of which were photographed for this chapter. They are extremely scarce and avidly sought after by collectors. (The "Howdy Doody" cookie jar was made expressly for Taylor, Smith, and Taylor and appears in Chapter 13).

The Purintons supplied local gift shops and restaurants with souvenirs of their lovely state parks and recreation areas. Several examples bearing names such as "Cook Forest State Park" and the "Pennsylvania Grand Canyon" appear in this chapter. Also sold in local gift shops was a wide variety of miniature items. Beware the authenticity of miniature pieces that are unmarked unless they are pictured here. Also illustrated are several examples of Kay Kraft jewelry which were fashioned by Kay Purinton, Bernard's daughter-in-law.

This chapter is a guide in which examples of Purinton's innovative shapes and patterns are illustrated. It is by no means a complete listing of all pieces made, but an attempt to familiarize the collector or dealer with a variety of pieces available.

CRESCENT FLOWER
Dutch Jug
2 pint, 5¾" high
$75.00

CRESCENT FLOWER
Handled Vase
7½" high
$125.00

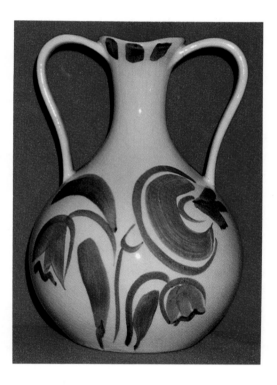

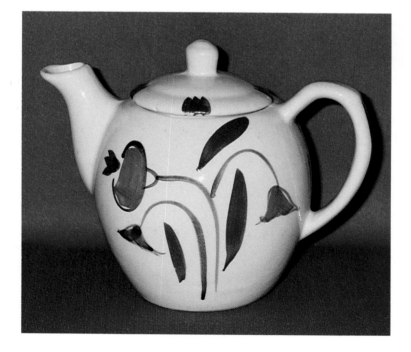

CRESCENT FLOWER
6-cup Teapot
6" high
$85.00

CRESCENT FLOWER
Breakfast Plate
(Old style — probably
done in Wellsville.)
8½" diameter
$55.00

CRESCENT FLOWER
Breakfast Plate
8½" diameter
$35.00

CRESCENT FLOWER
Lap Plate
8½" diameter
$35.00

CRESCENT FLOWER
Tumbler
12 oz.
5" high
$30.00

CRESCENT FLOWER
Tall Oil or Vinegar Bottle
9½" high, each $55.00

CRESCENT FLOWER Coaster
3½" diameter, $40.00

CRESCENT FLOWER Jar
3½" high, $45.00

CRESCENT FLOWER Round Shakers
2¾" high, pair $65.00

SEAFORM
Dinner Plate, 10" diameter, $25.00
Salad Plate, 7" diameter, $20.00
Dessert Bowl, 4" diameter, $20.00
Cup, 3¾" diameter, $20.00
Saucer, 5½" diameter, $8.00

SEAFORM
Meat Platter, 12" diameter, $50.00
Roll Tray, 11" long, $45.00

SEAFORM Divided Vegetable
10½" long, $50.00

SEAFORM Coffee Server
9" high
$125.00

Two Styles of SEAFORM Tidbit Trays
Each 10" diameter, 9" high, $75.00

SEAFORM
Salt and Pepper
3" high
pair $55.00

SEAFORM
Sugar and Creamer
5" high
set $85.00

154

TEA ROSE
Dinner Plate
9¾" diameter
$25.00
Breakfast Plate
8½" diameter, $25.00
Salad Plate
6¾" diameter, $20.00
Dessert Bowl
4" diameter, $20.00
Cup
2½" high, $20.00
Saucer
5½" diameter, $8.00

TEA ROSE
Meat Platter
12" diameter
$50.00

TEA ROSE
Roll Tray
11" long
$50.00

TEA ROSE
Covered Sugar, 5" high
Creamer, 3½" high
set $85.00

TEA ROSE
Miniature Jug-style Salt and Pepper
2½" high
pair $50.00

TEA ROSE
Open Vegetable
8½" diameter
$40.00

156

TEA ROSE Planter
5" high
$65.00

TEA ROSE Pitcher (Variation)
6½" high
This unusual pitcher was not
an open stock mold.
$100.00

TEA ROSE Variation
Sugar and Creamer on Tray
5" high, tray 9" long
This unusual set not only is
a rare variation of the TEA
ROSE pattern, but it was
painted on a SEAFORM
mold. See page 154.
$125.00

MOUNTAIN ROSE
Chop Plate (left)
12" diameter, $50.00
Dinner Plate
9¾" diameter, $25.00

MOUNTAIN ROSE
Tea and Toast
Lap Plate, 8½" diameter
$30.00
Cup, 2½" high
$20.00

MOUNTAIN ROSE
Miniature Sugar and Creamer
2" high
set $50.00

MOUNTAIN ROSE
Fruit Bowl
12" diameter
$55.00

MOUNTAIN ROSE
Covered Dish
9" long
$75.00

MOUNTAIN ROSE
Marmalade Jar, 4½" high
Bean Pot, 3¾" high
each $65.00

MOUNTAIN ROSE
Covered Range Bowl
5½" high, $65.00

MOUNTAIN ROSE
Kent Jug
1 pint, 4½" high, $45.00

MOUNTAIN ROSE
Three-Section Relish
10" diameter
$75.00

MOUNTAIN ROSE
Creamer
3½" high
Covered Sugar
5" high
Lid missing on
photographed
sugar.
set $85.00

160

MOUNTAIN ROSE
Jug, 5 pint, 8" high, $100.00
Tumblers, 12 oz., 5" high, each $35.00
(Note variation in leaves on front right tumbler.)

MOUNTAIN ROSE Dutch Jug
2 pint, 5¾" high
$85.00

MOUNTAIN ROSE
2-cup Teapot, 4" high, $45.00
4-cup Teapot, 5" high, $75.00

MOUNTAIN ROSE 6-cup Teapot
6½" high, $85.00

MOUNTAIN ROSE
Decanter
5" high, $45.00

MOUNTAIN ROSE
Wall Pocket, 3½" high, $65.00
Rum Jug Planter, 6½" high, $65.00

MOUNTAIN ROSE
Basket Planter
6¼" high, $50.00

MOUNTAIN ROSE
Rebecca Jug
7½" high, $45.00

MOUNTAIN ROSE
Oval-Shaped Cookie Jar
9½" high
$100.00

MOUNTAIN ROSE
Square-shaped Cookie Jar with Wooden Lid
9½" high
$100.00

PETALS
Dinner Plate, 9¾" diameter, $20.00
Breakfast Plate, 8½" diameter, $15.00
Juice Mug, 6 oz., 2½" high, $15.00
Cup, 2½" high, $15.00
Saucer, 5½" diameter, $6.00

PETALS
Fruit Bowl
12" diameter
$50.00

PETALS
Baker
7" diameter
$35.00

PETALS
Covered Dish
9" long
$65.00

PETALS
Miniature Jug-style
Salt and Pepper
2½" high
pair $40.00

166

PETALS 8-cup Coffee Pot
8" high
$75.00

PETALS
2-cup Teapot
4" high
$45.00

PETALS
Jug, 5 pint, 8" high, $85.00
Tumblers, 12 oz., 5" high, each $30.00
Juice Mugs, 6 oz., 2½" high, each $15.00

PETALS Beverage Pitcher
2 pint, 6¼" high, $75.00

PETALS
Honey Jug
6¼" high
$45.00

PETALS Vase
5" high
(With a lid this mold
doubled as a grease jar.)
$35.00

PETALS
Cookie Jar
9" high
$85.00

CHARTREUSE
Chop Plate
12" diameter
$25.00

CHARTREUSE Grill Platter
12" diameter
$30.00

CHARTREUSE
Cup, 2½" high, $10.00
Saucer, 5½" diameter, $3.00

CHARTREUSE
Rum Jug Planter
6½" high, $45.00

CHARTREUSE
Wall Pocket
3½" high, $35.00

CHARTREUSE
Covered Sugar
5" high, $30.00
Creamer
3½" high, $20.00

171

CHARTREUSE
Covered Dish
9" long
$55.00

CHARTREUSE
Open Vegetable
8½" diameter
$25.00

CHARTREUSE
Three-Section Relish
10" diameter
$45.00

CHARTREUSE
Tall Oil and Vinegar Bottles
1 pint, 9½" high
pair $75.00

CHARTREUSE
Range-style Salt and Pepper
4" high
pair $45.00

CHARTREUSE
Miniature Jug-style Salt and Pepper
2½" high, pair $30.00
Miniature Sugar and Creamer
2" high, set $40.00

CHARTREUSE
Dutch Jug, 2 pint, 5¾" high, $55.00
Juice Mugs, 6 oz., 2½" high, each $15.00

CHARTREUSE
Jug, 5 pint, 8" high, $75.00
Tumblers, 12 oz., 5" high, each $20.00

CHARTREUSE
Beverage Pitcher
2 pint, 6¼" high
$65.00

CHARTREUSE
8-cup Coffee Pot
8" high
$75.00

CHARTREUSE Oval-shaped Cookie Jar
9½" high
$75.00

CHARTREUSE Oval-shaped Canister Set (Tea missing)
9" high, each $60.00

✥ Ming Tree ✥

MING TREE Meat Platter
12" diameter
$40.00

MING TREE Chop Plate
12" diameter
$35.00

MING TREE Dinner Plate
9¾" diameter
$20.00

MING TREE
Dinner Plate
9¾" diameter, $20.00
Cup
2½" high, $15.00
Saucer
5½" diameter, $5.00

MING TREE
2-cup Teapot
5" high, $55.00
6-cup Teapot
6½" high, $75.00

MING TREE Canister
Variation of original pattern
7½" high
$65.00

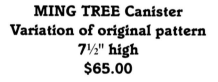

MING TREE Planter
5" high
$35.00

MING TREE Jardiniere
5" high
$40.00

MING TREE Pillow Vases
4¼" high (left), $35.00
6½" high, $45.00

IVY – RED BLOSSOM
6-cup Teapot with
Drip Filter (left)
9" high, $75.00
8-cup Coffee Pot
with Drip Filter
11" high, $85.00

IVY – RED BLOSSOM
2-cup Teapot, 4" high, $45.00
4-cup Teapot, 5" high, $55.00
6-cup Teapot, 6" high, $55.00

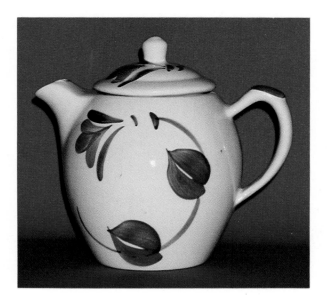

IVY – RED BLOSSOM
Coffee Pot
8" high, $65.00

IVY – RED BLOSSOM
Kent Jug
1 pint, 4½" high
$30.00

IVY – RED BLOSSOM
Juice Mug
6 oz., 2½" high
$15.00

IVY – RED BLOSSOM
Dutch Jug
2 pint, 5¾" high
$45.00

IVY – RED BLOSSOM
Beverage Pitcher
2 pint, 6¼" high
$55.00

IVY – RED BLOSSOM
Miniature Jug-style Salt and Pepper
2½" high
pair $20.00

IVY – RED BLOSSOM
Miniature Creamer and Sugar
2" high
set $30.00

IVY – RED BLOSSOM
Miniature Decanter
(no holes on top)
2½" high
$12.00

IVY – RED BLOSSOM
Covered Sugar, 5" high, $25.00
Creamer, 3½" high, $15.00

IVY – RED BLOSSOM
Cookie Jar
9½" high, $75.00

IVY – RED BLOSSOM
Biscuit Jar
8" high, $55.00

IVY – RED BLOSSOM
Range-style Salt and Pepper, 4" high, pair $40.00
Covered Range Bowl, 5½" high, $45.00

IVY – RED BLOSSOM Jardinieres (NAPCO molds)
4¼" high, $20.00
5½" high, $30.00

IVY – BLUE AND RED BLOSSOMS
Jardiniere (NAPCO mold)
5" high, $30.00

IVY – RED BLOSSOM
Cornucopia Vase
6" high
$25.00

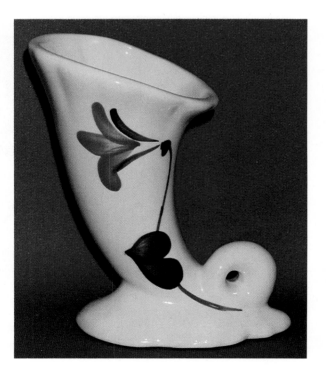

**IVY –
YELLOW BLOSSOM**
Covered Sugar
5" high, $25.00
Creamer
3½" high, $15.00

**IVY –
YELLOW BLOSSOM**
2-cup Teapot
4" high, $35.00
6-cup Teapot
6" high, $45.00

IVY – YELLOW BLOSSOM
8-cup Coffee Pot
8" high
$50.00

187

IVY – YELLOW BLOSSOM
Kent Jug
1 pint, 4½" high
$30.00

IVY – YELLOW BLOSSOM
Honey Jug
6¼" high
$35.00

IVY – YELLOW BLOSSOM
Dutch Jug
2 pint, 5¾" high
$45.00

DAISY Oval-shaped Canister Set (Cobalt Trim)
9" high, each $75.00

DAISY Tea Canister (Red Trim)
9" high
each $60.00

DAISY Tall Oil and Vinegar Bottles
1 pint, 9½" high
pair $75.00

189

DAISY Range-style Salt and Pepper (Red trim)
4" high, pair $50.00

DAISY Rebecca Jug
7½" high, $50.00

DAISY Covered Grease Jar
5½" high, $60.00

DAISY Range-style
Salt and Pepper
(Cobalt trim) 4" high
pair $50.00
Covered Grease Jar
5½" high, $30.00

PALM TREE Dinner Plate
9¾" diameter, $125.00

PALM TREE Vase
5" high, $75.00

PALM TREE Basket Planter
6¼" high, $100.00

PALM TREE Mug Jug
8 oz., 4¾" high, $100.00

PALM TREE Canister
9½" high
$175.00

PALM TREE Marmalade Jar
4½" high, $125.00

PALM TREE
Pour 'N Shake Salt and Pepper, 4½" high, pair $150.00
Miniature Jug-style Salt and Pepper, 2½" high, pair $85.00
Range-style Salt and Pepper, 4" high, pair $125.00

PALM TREE Beverage Pitcher
2 pint, 6¼" high
$150.00

PALM TREE Beer Mug
16 oz., 4¾" high
$85.00

PALM TREE Dutch Jug
2 pint, 5¾" high
$150.00

PALM TREE Honey Jug
6¼" high
$125.00

WOODFLOWERS
Covered Sugar, 4" high, $45.00
Pitcher, 6½" high, $65.00
Relish Tray, 8" long, $45.00

STARFLOWER
Pitchers, 5½", 6", and 6½" high, each $65.00
Creamer, 4½" high, and Covered Sugar, 4" high, set $85.00
Relish Tray, 8" long, $45.00

Book Decanters (Set of three on original metal rack)
Each decanter 7¾" high
set $125.00

RED FEATHER TV Lamp
(Popular item with the advent
of television in the 50's.)
8½" high, $75.00

Clarion Chapter Eastern Star Plate
7" diameter
$55.00

Ashtray
6" diameter
$50.00

INTAGLIO – Style Ashtray
6" diameter
$75.00

INTAGLIO – Style
Blindman's Ashtray
(Patent was applied for on this mold.)
4½" long
$75.00

INTAGLIO – Style
Candleholders in Brown,
Aqua, and Coral
6" diameter, 2" high
each $55.00

SPATTERWARE
Beer Mug
16 oz., 4¾" high, $25.00
Blindman's Ashtray
(Patent was applied
for on this mold.)
4½" long, $40.00

Green Beer Mug (MAYWOOD glaze)
16 oz., 4¾" high
$20.00

**Turquoise and Yellow
Water Bottles
9" high
each $35.00**

**Turquoise, Yellow, and White Juice Mugs
6 oz., 2½" high, each $10.00
Yellow Butter Dish
6½" long, $25.00
Yellow Dutch Jug
2 pint, 5¾" high, $25.00**

**Black and White Stacking
Salt and Pepper
2¼" high
pair $15.00**

Cornucopia Vases in Miscellaneous Floral Patterns 6" high each $25.00

Cornucopia Vases in Miscellaneous Floral Patterns 6" high each $25.00

Vases in Miscellaneous Floral Patterns 5" high each $25.00

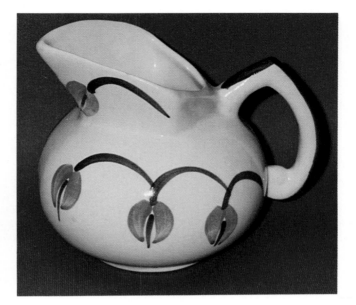

FUSCHIA Kent Jug
1 pint, 4½" high
$35.00

SHOOTING STAR Honey Jug
6¼" high
$35.00

SHOOTING STAR
Vases
5" high, $25.00
6" high, $30.00

WINDFLOWER Jardiniere
5" high
$30.00

WINDFLOWER Honey Jug
6¼" high
$40.00

HALF-BLOSSOM
Rum Jug Planter
6½" high, $55.00

HALF-BLOSSOM Vase
5" high
$25.00

Miscellaneous Wall Pockets in Various Floral Patterns
3½" high
Center, $65.00, others each $40.00

MORNING GLORY Honey Jug
6¼" high
$50.00

BLUE PANSY Basket Planter
6¼" high
$65.00

DECO-STYLE Wall Pocket
3½" high
$55.00

**SUNNY Jardiniere on
Wrought Iron Stand**
$30.00

**SUNNY
Jardiniere (NAPCO mold)**
5" high, $25.00
Wall Pocket
3½" high, $40.00

YELLOW TULIP
Sprinkler Planter
5½" high
(This is a mold originally produced for National Potteries Inc. [NAPCO] but many were hand decorated and sold by Purinton.)
$60.00

RED TULIP Sprinkler Planter
5½" high
$65.00

LEAVES Sprinkler Planter
5½" high
$50.00

LEAVES Jardiniere
5" high
$25.00

LEAVES Planter
3" high
$30.00

LEAVES Square-shaped Canister
(Same mold used without lid
is called a pillow vase.)
5½" high, each $40.00

LEAVES Table Lamp
6¼" high (pottery section)
$65.00

Square Planter
5¼" high
$25.00

PINE TREE Jardiniere
5" high
$40.00

PEASANT HOUSE Candy Dish (NAPCO mold)
6" long
$60.00

❧ Teapots ❧

YELLOW GLAZE Individual 2-cup Teapot
(Also made in deep turquoise and brown.)
This was Purinton's first teapot. The first
100 made were inscribed on the bottom
"12-2-41 B.P." by Bernard Purinton.
4" high
No inscription, $25.00
Inscribed by Bernard Purinton, $50.00

ORIENTAL – STYLE
Individual
2-cup Teapot
4" high
(Used as a premium
for selling tea.)
each $35.00

ROSEBUDS Teapot (rare mold)
5¾" high
$85.00

BLUE PANSY 6-cup Teapot (rare mold)
5¾" high, $125.00

THREE PANSIES 6-cup Teapot (rare mold)
5¾" high, $125.00

CHERRIES 2-cup Teapot
4" high
$50.00

CHERRIES 6-cup Teapot
(Rare mold)
5¾" high
$125.00

FEATHER FLOWER
2-cup Teapot
4" high
$55.00

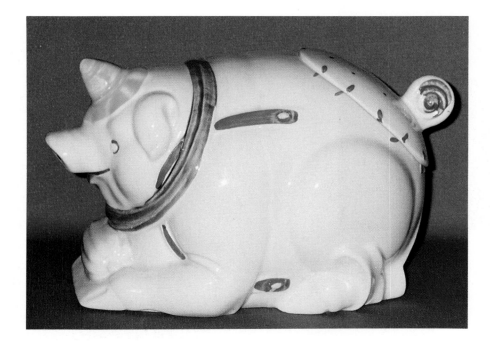

PIG WITH CORN COB
Cookie Jar
7" high, 11½" long
$450.00+

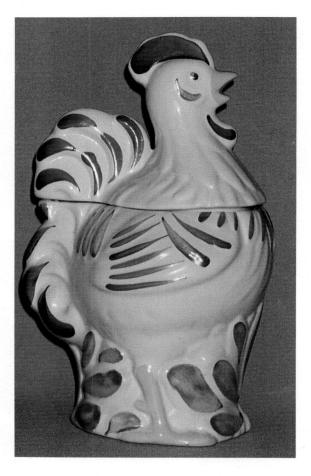

HUMPTY DUMPTY Cookie Jar
10" high, 8¼" wide
$450.00+

ROOSTER Cookie Jar
11" high
$400.00+

✃ Souvenir Items ✃

COOK FOREST Souvenir Chop Plate
(Hand signed on back by D. Purinton.)
12" diameter
signed $300.00+

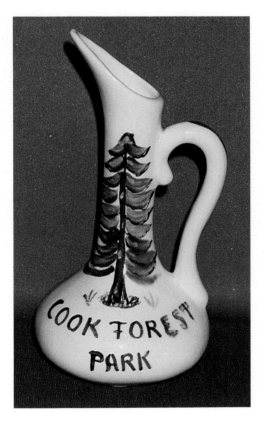

COOK FOREST Souvenir Ewer
9" high
$150.00

COOK FOREST Souvenir
Stacking Salt and Pepper
2¼" high
pair $100.00

PENNSYLVANIA Souvenir Plate
(Hand signed "D. Purinton.")
9¾" diameter
Signed $300.00+

PENNSYLVANIA GRAND CANYON
Souvenir Ewer
9" high
$125.00

ALPHA CHALET
Souvenir Plate
9¾" diameter
$175.00+

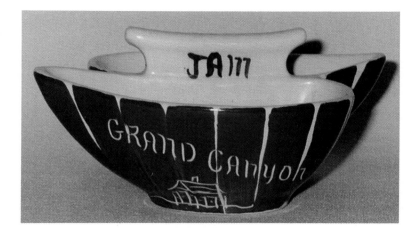

PENNSYLVANIA GRAND CANYON
Souvenir Jam and Jelly Dish
INTAGLIO-Style
5½" long
$75.00

CLARION Souvenir Stacking Salt and Pepper
INTAGLIO-Style
2¼" high
pair $85.00

PENNSYLVANIA GRAND CANYON
Souvenir Honey Jug, INTAGLIO-Style
6¼" high, $85.00

COOK FOREST
Souvenir Kent Jug
INTAGLIO-Style
1 pint, 4½" high
PENNSYLVANIA
Souvenir Handled Mug
INTAGLIO-Style
8 oz., 4" high
each $75.00

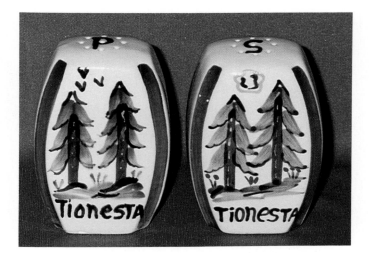

TIONESTA PARK
Souvenir Range-style Salt and Pepper
4" high
pair $125.00

COOK FOREST PARK
Souvenir Range-style
Salt and Pepper
4" high, pair $125.00
CLEAR CREEK
Souvenir Mug Jug
8 oz., 4¾" high
$100.00

AUTUMN LEAF FESTIVAL Souvenir Plates (Hand signed on back by Dorothy Purinton.)
9¾" diameter, each $250.00+ (signed)

BOOT
4½" high, $10.00
LADIES' SHOE
3¼" long, $15.00

DUTCH SHOES
4" – 5" long
each $5.00 – $10.00

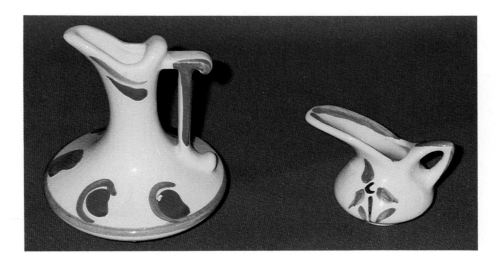

Miniature Ewer (left)
4" high, $15.00
Miniature Dutch Jug
2" high, $10.00

Toothpick Holder
5" long, $25.00
Shaker
5" long, $25.00

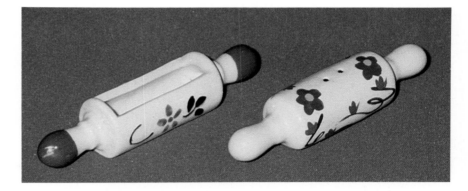

OLD SALT AND
PEPPER HIS WIFE
(Two variations of this
rare salt and pepper set.)
3" high, pair $125.00

Horse and Dog
Figurines
6½" high
each $25.00

Miniature PIGGY BANKS
4" long
each $25.00

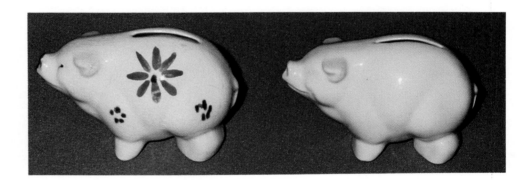

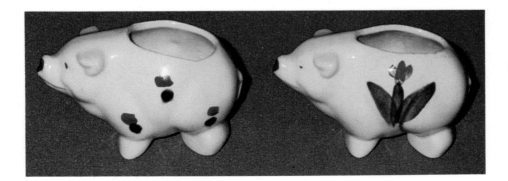

Miniature PIG PLANTERS
4" long
each $25.00

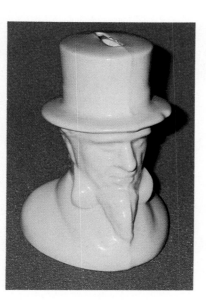

UNCLE SAM Banks
4½" high
each $50.00

OWL Bank
3¼" high
$35.00

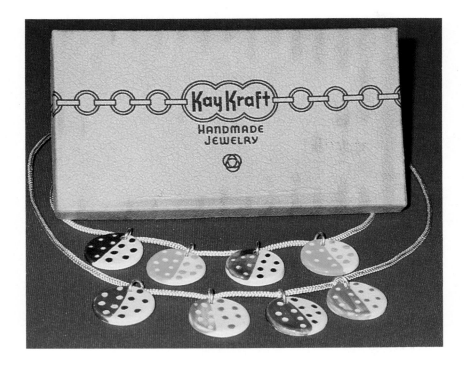

KAY KRAFT Polka Dot Necklaces (in original box)
each $45.00

KAY KRAFT Floral Necklaces
each $60.00

KAY KRAFT
Charm Bracelets and Miscellaneous Charms
each $20.00

KAY KRAFT Charm Bracelet
(Note the PALM TREE and PLAID patterns.)
$50.00

Chapter 12

⥈ Unusual and Unique Items ⥈

Because the Purintons encouraged individuality and ingenuity in the decorating division of their operation, many unusual and unique creations emerged from their kilns. This chapter will illustrate a few examples of these rarities, however, the collector should become acquainted with Purinton's molds, color usage, and style to be able to identify a rare or unique piece.

Pictured in this chapter are some items produced with common molds, but hand-painted with rare and unusual patterns. Many are experimental pieces made while attempting to invent new pattern lines and were produced in very limited numbers. Others may be the only one of its kind. Also photographed are many unusual pieces made with molds that never became part of a regular production line.

Especially rare and desirable are the Christmas pieces which were produced in extremely limited numbers. Most were distributed locally as giftware. Hand-painted plates were a specialty of both Dorothy Purinton and William Blair and a wide variety of their efforts were photographed for this chapter. Especially prized by collectors are the Peasant scenes and the traditional "blessing" verses depicting the Pennsylvania Dutch heritage of this region. Most of these special plates are hand signed on the back by Dorothy Purinton or William Blair.

The rare and unusual examples of Purinton pottery, especially those that bear the artist's signature, are avidly sought after by collectors. The beauty and individuality of these treasured pieces are fine examples of the Purinton tradition.

PEASANT Chop Plate
(Hand signed by Dorothy
Purinton "Purinton Pottery.")
12" diameter
signed $350.00+

PEASANT Vase
6" high, $125.00

PENNSYLVANIA DUTCH Style Dinner Plate
(Hand signed "Dorothy Purinton.")
9¾" diameter
signed $300.00+

AMISH COUPLE Chop Plate
(Hand signed "Dorothy Purinton
1954" on back.)
12" diameter
signed $350.00+

Unusual Hand-painted Fruit Bowl
(Hand signed
"Purinton Pottery" on back.)
12" diameter
signed $125.00

AMISH CHILDREN
Chop Plate
(Hand signed
"D. Purinton" on back.)
12" diameter
signed $350.00+

Unusual 4-cup Teapot
5" high
$125.00

Unusual Tumbler
(Hand signed "Blair.")
5" high
signed $100.00

Dorie's Handled Mug
(Made for Doris Purinton.)
4" high, $100.00

Unusual Tumbler
5" high
$75.00

PENNSYLVANIA DUTCH Style Blessing Plate
(Hand signed "Dorothy Purinton 1954.") 12" diameter, signed $350.00+

PENNSYLVANIA DUTCH Style Blessing Plate
(Rubel mold, hand signed "Dorothy Purinton — Hand Painted.")
14" diameter, signed $350.00+

PENNSYLVANIA DUTCH Style Blessing Plate
(Hand signed "Dorothy Purinton.")
11" diameter, signed $350.00+

FRUITS Blessing Plate
(Hand signed "Dorothy Purinton.")
12" diameter, signed $300.00+

227

LOG CABIN Intaglio-style Plate
(Hand signed "D. Purinton, 1954, Hand Painted.")
6¾" diameter, signed $175.00+

LEAVES Plate
(Hand signed "HBP" by Harry "Blair" Purinton.)
8½" diameter, signed $150.00+

THISTLE Blessing Plate
(Hand signed "D. Purinton.")
12" diameter
signed $350.00+

Some hae meat
An can na eat
Some can eat
An hae na meat
But we hae meat
An we can eat
So Let the Lord
Be Thankit

PENNSYLVANIA DUTCH Style
Anniversary Plate
(Hand painted by Dorothy Purinton for her
son, Blair, and his wife, Doris. Hand signed on
back "Dorothy Purinton – October 15, 1959.")
12" diameter
signed $300.00+

PENNSYLVANIA DUTCH Style
Anniversary Plate
(Hand painted by Dorothy Purinton for
Bill Bower and his wife, Ardelle.
Hand signed on back "D. Purinton.")
12" diameter
signed $300.00+

INTAGLIO-Style Anniversary Plate
(Hand signed on back
"Best Wishes – Dot Purinton.")
12" diameter
signed $200.00+

Unusual Ashtray
3" high
$150.00

PORTRAIT OF A LADY Plate
(Hand signed "Wm. H. Blair — Purinton Pottery.")
12" diameter
signed $175.00+

Early Hand-painted Square Dish
(Probably an experimental piece
made at the Wellsville plant.)
8¾" diameter
$100.00

FRUITS AND LEAVES
Chop Plate
(An original design, hand
signed "Purinton Pottery
W.H. Blair.")
12" diameter
signed $250.00+

FRUITS Pitcher (Rubel mold)
(Hand signed "D. Purinton.")
Very few of these pitchers
were made.
8¼" high
signed $250.00+

LEAF Plate
9¾" diameter
$25.00

SWIRLS Plate
9¾" diameter
$25.00

HORSE AND CART Plate
9¾" diameter
$100.00

APPLE Blessing Plate
(Hand signed by Dorothy Purinton.)
9¾" diameter, signed $225.00+

Hand-painted Plate — experimental pattern
(Hand signed on back by Dorothy Purinton.)
SEAFORM Dinner Plate mold
10" diameter
signed $200.00+

Hand-painted Plate — experimental pattern
SEAFORM Dinner Plate mold
10" diameter
$55.00

Hand-painted Plate — experimental pattern
SEAFORM Dinner Plate mold
10" diameter
$55.00

**Hand-painted Plate — experimental pattern
SEAFORM Dinner Plate mold
10" diameter
$100.00**

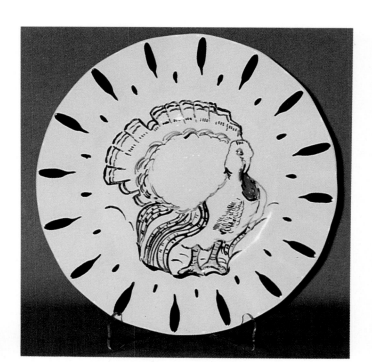

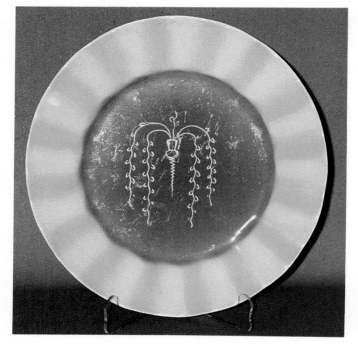

**Incised Design Experimental Plate
SEAFORM Dinner Plate mold
10" diameter
$40.00**

**Hand-painted Plate — experimental pattern
SEAFORM Dinner Plate mold
10" diameter
$30.00**

Purple INTAGLIO-Style Beer Mug
Rare PALM TREE pattern
16 oz., 4¾" high
$125.00+

Maroon INTAGLIO-Style Dinner Plate
Rare PALM TREE pattern
9¾" high
$125.00+

Blue INTAGLIO-Style Dinner Plate
Rare PALM TREE pattern
9¾" diameter
$125.00+

Turquoise INTAGLIO-Style Dinner Plate
Rare PALM TREE pattern
9¾" diameter
$125.00+

Turquoise INTAGLIO-Style, rare PALM TREE pattern
Cup, 2½" high, Saucer, 5½" diameter, set $50.00+
Creamer, 3½" high, $65.00+

Coral INTAGLIO-Style Dinner Plate
Rare PALM TREE pattern
9¾" diameter
$125.00+

Coral INTAGLIO-Style 6-cup Teapot
Rare PALM TREE pattern
6½" high
$150.00+

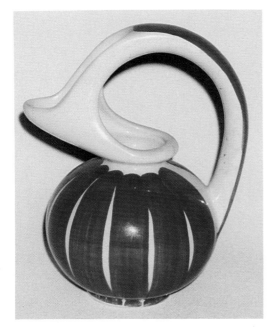

Coral INTAGLIO-Style Honey Jug
6¼" high
$60.00

Carmel INTAGLIO-Style Wedding Plate
(Hand painted by Dorothy Purinton for
her son, Blair, and his bride, Doris.
Hand signed on back "Love from Mom and
Pops for always — Dorothy Purinton.")
12" diameter
signed $200.00+

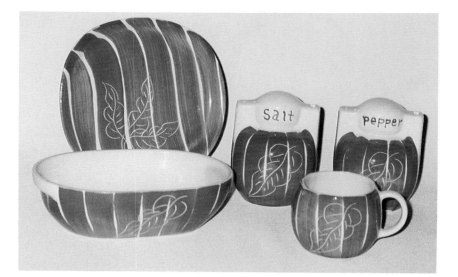

Carmel INTAGLIO-Style Plate
SEAFORM Dinner Plate mold
10" diameter
$45.00

Carmel INTAGLIO-Style
Probably an experimental line
Dinner Plate
9¾" diameter, $25.00
Pour 'N Shake Salt and Pepper
4¼" high, set $50.00
Baker
7" diameter, $30.00
Cup
2½" high, $15.00

238

INTAGLIO-Style CUPIDS Plate
9¾" diameter
$100.00

INTAGLIO-Style Vases
(Hand signed on bottom "Wm.
H. Blair — Purinton Pottery.")
6" high
each $100.00

239

INTAGLIO-Style DEER Plate
(Hand signed on back "Wm. H. Blair — Purinton Pottery.")
12" diameter
signed $100.00

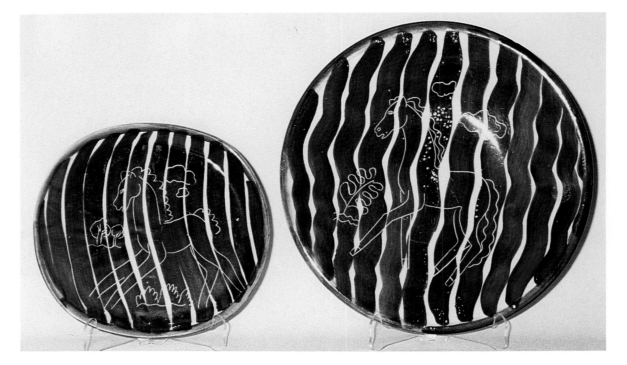

INTAGLIO-Style HORSE Plates
Left (Hand signed on back "Wm. H. Blair."), 8½" diameter
Right, 12" diameter
signed each $100.00

DONKEY Plate
(Stamped "Purinton Pottery.")
12" diameter, $75.00

ZEBRA Plate
(Hand signed "Wm. H. Blair — Purinton Pottery.)
12" diameter, signed $100.00

DEER Plate
(Hand signed "Wm. H. Blair" and stamped
"Purinton Pottery.")
12" diameter, signed $100.00

GIRAFFE Plate
(Stamped "Purinton Pottery.")
12" diameter, $75.00

DUCK Handled Mug
8 oz., 4" high
$100.00

DUCK Breakfast Plate
8½" diameter, $85.00

ELEPHANT Handled Mug
8 oz., 4" high
$100.00

KITTEN Breakfast Plate
8½" diameter, $85.00

LAMB Breakfast Plate
8½" diameter
$85.00

DOG Breakfast Plate
8½" diameter
$85.00

REINDEER Breakfast Plate
8½" diameter
$85.00

MERRY CHRISTMAS Plate
(Hand signed "D. Purinton 1953.")
9¾" diameter, signed $300.00+

HOLLY Jam and Jelly Dish
(Probably sold as a candy dish.)
5½" long
$80.00

PINE NEEDLES
Christmas Tree
6" high, $90.00

HOLLY Ashtray
5½" long
$65.00

HOLLY Bowl
8½" diameter
$65.00

HOLLY Covered Bowl
(Part of a Lazy Susan set,
Esmond mold)
8½" diameter, $100.00
Complete Lazy Susan,
$185.00

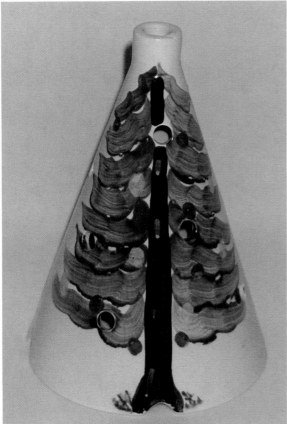

FIR TREE Christmas Tree
8" high, 5" diameter at base
$150.00

HOLLY Christmas Tree
8" high, 5" diameter at base
$125.00

The above Christmas Trees were made to cover a light or candle. Notice the groove at the base for the cord to pass through.

CHRISTMAS CANDLE Handled Mug
8 oz., 4" high
$125.00

SANTA Mug
(Marked NAPCO, made for National Potteries
Corporation of Cleveland, Ohio.)
5½" high, $75.00

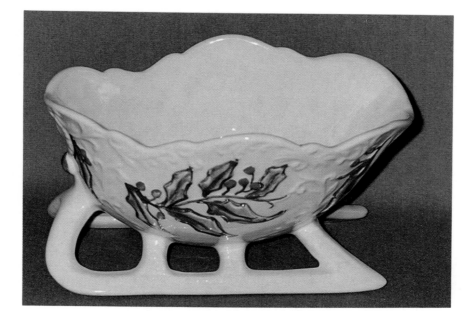

HOLLY Sled
(Bottom signed "Tionesta, PA 12-4-52" by Dorothy Purinton.)
8" long, signed $100.00

Very few of these pieces were made at the Tionesta plant. Beware of copies of this piece! We have seen similar unmarked pieces, probably made during the same time period, both 5" and 8" long that are decorated over the glaze. These versions are NOT Purinton Pottery. We assume that Dorothy signed all the pieces that she painted.

HOLLY Punch Set
(Very rare — only a few sets were made.)
Punch Bowl, 10½" diameter
Cups, 2½" high
set $300.00

Triangular Serving Dish
ABSTRACT Design
12" diameter, 3½" high
$150.00

Triangular Serving Dish
FRUIT Design
(Apple, Pear, Grapes)
12" diameter, 3½" high
$150.00

Triangular Pitcher
ABSTRACT Design
10½" high
$150.00

Unusual APPLE Vase
6" high
$65.00

Rare Two-Handled Vase
(Note similarities to
MOUNTAIN ROSE pattern.)
9" high, $85.00

Unusual Vases
(Note that the center vase is the night bottle mold with handles
applied and painted with the HOWDY DOODY colors.)
7½" – 9" high
Center vase, $75.00, others each $50.00

WATER SCENE Night Bottle
7½" high, $100.00

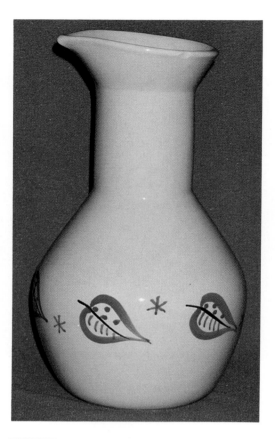

AUTUMN LEAVES Bulbous Pitcher
9½" high, $45.00

Spoons Holder
6" high, $85.00

Forks Holder
7¼" high, $85.00

Bell-shaped Pitcher
8" high
$90.00

Square-shaped Pitcher
(Made to hold a milk carton.)
7" high $85.00

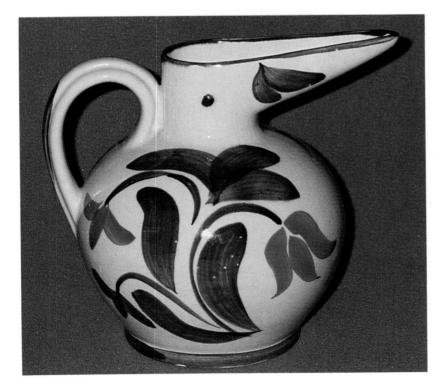

BIRD Pitcher
7" high
$185.00

MORNING GLORY Blessing Plate
(Hand signed "D. Purinton.")
12" diameter, signed $300.00+

MORNING GLORY Cookie Jar
9½" high, $150.00

HARMONY Oval-shaped Cookie Jar
9½" high
$75.00

HARMONY
6-cup Teapot, 6½" high, $65.00
Creamer, 3½" high, $30.00
Covered Sugar, 5" high, $35.00

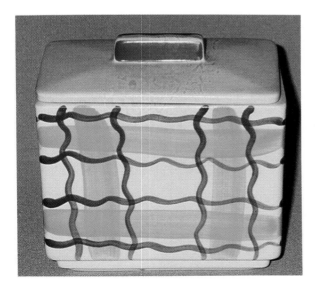

CHARTREUSE PLAID Square Canister
Experimental pattern
5½" high, $35.00

253

CARMEL PLAID 6-cup Teapot
Experimental pattern
6" high, $65.00

PURPLE PLAID
Experimental pattern
Cup, 2½" high
Saucer, 5½" diameter
set $35.00

AUTUMN LEAVES
Creamer and Sugar
4¾" high
set $35.00

Oval-shaped Canisters with
Experimental Designs
(Lids missing)
7½" high, each $50.00

254

Chapter 13

❧ Pottery Made for Other Companies ❧

The Purinton Pottery Company contracted a considerable amount of private mold work for other companies. Many of these pieces would not be important to a Purinton collector as they were undecorated, but there is a wide array of hand-painted items that are particularly desirable and unique. This chapter attempts to familiarize the dealer or collector with a few examples of this ware which was made for four different companies: Esmond Industries, Inc.; National Potteries Corporation (NAPCO); Taylor, Smith, and Taylor (TS & T); and the Rubel Company.

Esmond Industries, Inc. was based in New York City and contracted Purinton to produce lazy susan sets, condiment sets on wire racks, covered casseroles on wire racks, cookie jars, and revolving canister sets. It is important to note that Purinton originally designed the straight-sided revolving canister set with a wood base and lid (see page 256) and produced it as part of their own line as well as for sale by Esmond. Esmond never produced pottery of their own, but contracted with many other companies to produce their products. The collector of Purinton must be careful to use information contained in this chapter as well as Chapter 14 on bottom markings to differentiate between Esmond pieces produced by companies other than Purinton.

National Potteries Corporation (NAPCO) of Cleveland, Ohio contracted much work from Purinton in the florist container line. Their popular "pillow vase" mold eventually was adapted by Purinton for use in producing their square canisters.

Purinton produced various animal figurines in different colored glazes as well as many other products for Taylor, Smith & Taylor (TS & T) of Chester, West Virginia, but the most important line made for this company was the Howdy Doody. The distinctive Howdy Doody cookie jar and bank were made at the Tionesta plant. Although the cookie jar was produced rather heavily, the bank was sent out in very limited numbers. These items are highly collectible and command premium prices. Some of TS & T's ware was hand-painted with tulip motifs and photographs of these lovely pieces appear in this chapter.

A few examples of undecorated ware which were made for the Rubel Company of New York are illustrated in this chapter for identification purposes. As was stated earlier, pieces made with private molds are only important to a Purinton collector if they are artist-decorated.

It is interesting to note that many of the molds were designed for the above-mentioned companies can be found decorated with Purinton patterns. Pieces of this type, examples of which are pointed out throughout this text, were most likely distributed locally and were not part of a regular production line.

Frontal view of each section in revolving canister set pictured below.

FRUIT Straight-sided Four-Section Canister Set on Revolving Wooden Base
Also came in Flour, Sugar, Coffee, and Tea
Made for Esmond Industries, Inc.
Each section 7" high
$125.00

Frontal view of each section in revolving canister set pictured below.

FRUIT Bulbous-Shaped Four-Section Canister Set on Revolving Wooden Base
Made for Esmond Industries, Inc.
Each section 7" high
$125.00

FRUIT Four-Section Long Canister Set on Wire Carrier (Wooden Lid)
Made for Esmond Industries, Inc.
19" long, $175.00

FRUIT Bulbous Cookie Jar
Made for Esmond Industries, Inc.
9" high
$75.00

FRUIT Lazy Susan on Revolving Wooden Base
Made for Esmond Industries, Inc.
17" diameter
$125.00

MOUNTAIN FLOWERS Lazy Susan on Revolving Wooden Base
Made for Esmond Industries, Inc.
17" diameter
$125.00

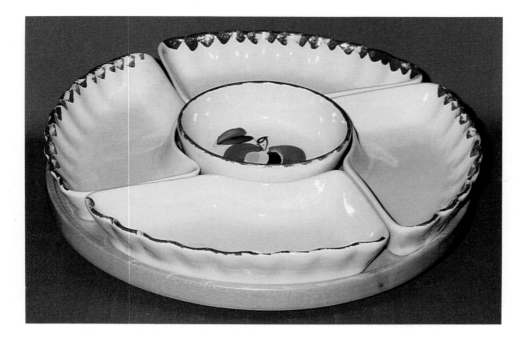

APPLE Lazy Susan on Revolving Wooden Base
Made for Esmond Industries, Inc.
13" diameter
$85.00

BIG TOP Lazy Susan on Revolving Wooden Base
Made for Esmond Industries, Inc.
17" diameter
$150.00

FRUIT Condiment Set on Wire Rack
Square-shaped Oil and Vinegar
Cruets, 5" tall
Salt and Pepper (SEAFORM
mold), 3" high
Made for Esmond Industries, Inc.
set $125.00

FRUIT Twin Casserole Set on Wire Stand
Casserole Lid, 8½" diameter
Casserole bottom, 7½" diameter
Stand, 19" long
Made for Esmond Industries, Inc.
$125.00

Box for Twin Casserole Set

TULIP AND VINE Coffee Server
10½" high
Made for Taylor, Smith, and Taylor.
$100.00

TULIP AND BUDS Coffee Server
10½" high
Made for Taylor, Smith, and Taylor.
$125.00

TULIP AND VINE
Tureen, sometimes sold on wire warming stand, 6½" high, $85.00
Gravy Boat, 3¾" high, $65.00
Made for Taylor, Smith, and Taylor.

HOWDY DOODY Cookie Jar
9" high
Made for Taylor, Smith, and Taylor.
$650.00+

HOWDY DOODY Bank
8" high
Made for Taylor, Smith, and Taylor.
$800.00+

SQUIRREL Figurine
Left, 6½" high, $100.00
Below, 11" long, $100.00
Made for Taylor, Smith, and Taylor.

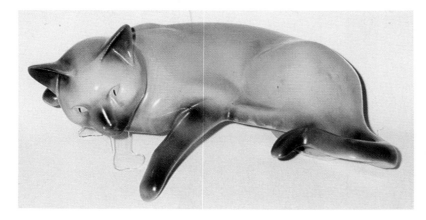

COUCH CAT Figurines
13" long, each $150.00
Made for Taylor, Smith, and Taylor.
These figurines were made to rest on
the top of a couch.

Water Bottle, 9" high, $25.00
Ramekin, 7½" long, $10.00
Made for Taylor, Smith, and
Taylor.

Stick-Handled Baker
14" long
Made for Taylor, Smith, and Taylor.
$10.00

INTAGLIO-Style
Console Bowl, 11" long
Made for NAPCO — National Potteries Corporation
$65.00

LEAVES Sprinker Planter
5½" high, $50.00
Made for NAPCO —
National Potteries
Corporation

IVY — RED BLOSSOM Jardinieres
4¼" high, $20.00, 5½" high, $30.00
Made for NAPCO — National Potteries Corporation

INTAGLIO-Style
Rectangular Planter
7" long, $35.00
Made for NAPCO —
National Potteries
Corporation

Black and White Rubel Ware
Stick-Handled Casserole, 13½" long, $10.00
Covered Casserole, 13½" long, $20.00
Made for Rubel Company.

Yellow and Brown Rubel Ware
Stick-Handled Casserole, 8" long, $15.00
Mixing Bowl, 5¾" diameter, $10.00
Made for Rubel Company.

Rubel Salad Bowl
13½" diameter, $15.00
Made for Rubel Company.

Chapter 14

Company Markings
❧ on Purinton Slip Ware ❧

A large percentage of Purinton's ware did not bear company bottom markings, making it difficult to identify without becoming familiar with their molds, pattern decorations, and color usage. However, many pieces bear a stamped identification which was imprinted in usually dark brown, sometimes teal, on the bottom or back. The brown-colored imprint was usually stamped "Purinton Slip Ware" or "Purinton Slip Ware Hand Painted" and the less commonly used teal-colored mark was usually stamped "Purinton Pottery." Few pieces bear an incised impression in block letters, "PURINTON SLIP WARE" on the bottom or an artist signed, usually script, mark "Purinton Pottery" in dark brown slip.

Individualized pieces with unique artwork were usually signed, and sometimes dated, under the glaze by either Dorothy Purinton or William Blair. These pieces are rare and highly collectible.

Pieces made for Esmond Industries Inc. may bear a tiny brown stamp under the glaze stating "Esmond," "Esmond U.S.A.," "U.S.A.," or an incised impression "USA," however, many pieces were unmarked. Because Purinton designed and sold the revolving canister sets under their own name as well, unmarked pieces or those simply marked "U.S.A." may not have been sold under the Esmond name. Other pottery companies made ware for Esmond and pieces marked with patent numbers, copyright symbols, or mold numbers are not Purinton-made.

Molds designed by the Rubel Company and made by Purinton usually bear an incised impression "Rubel" and a mold number. Ware made for National Potteries Corporation usually bore the incised mark "NAPCO Cleveland O." Pieces made for Taylor, Smith, and Taylor were unmarked. Many square-shaped canister bottoms and pillow vases (same molds) bear the incised mark "Norton Pillow #1" and "Norton Pillow #2." These are molds initially made for NAPCO to be used for vases. However, Purinton eventually was permitted to use these molds for their handpainted square-shaped canister set with lids and the decorated pillow vases in their florist line. Keep in mind that pieces bearing "Rubel" or "NAPCO" marks are only important to a Purinton collector if they are free brush decorated.

Photographs and illustrations of the above-described marks found on Purinton pottery are listed on the following pages. Variations of Dorothy Purinton's and William Blair's signatures were photographed to aid the collector in identifying authentic hand-signed pieces.

Purinton
SLIP WARE

Purinton Logos

**ESMOND
U.S.A.**   **U.S.A.**   **USA**   *Rubel*

                                                     2008

Esmond Backstamps   **Esmond Incised Mark**   **Rubel Incised Mark**
(Brown)

NAPCO

USA

CLEVELAND, O

NAPCO Incised Mark   Norton Pillow #2

                              **NAPCO Incised Mark found
                              on Pillow Vases and Square-
                              shaped Canisters**

Purinton Bottom Markings

BACKSTAMPS

(Usually brown)

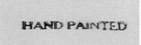

(Usually teal)

HAND PAINTED

(Usually brown)

UNKOWN ARTIST MARKINGS

(Usually brown)

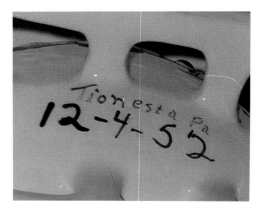

Mark found on bottom of Christmas Sleigh Planter on page 247. Probably done by Dorothy Purinton.

Incised Mark

Examples of Dorothy Purinton's Hand Signed Bottom Markings
(Usually done in dark brown, sometimes teal.)

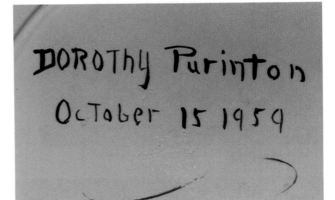

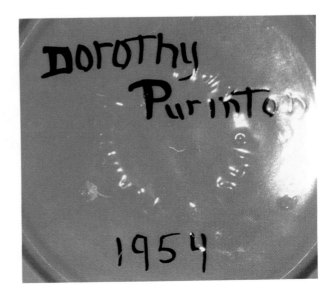